6⁰⁰

TWAYNE'S WORLD AUTHORS SERIES
A Survey of the World's Literature

Sylvia E. Bowman, Indiana University

GENERAL EDITOR

SPAIN

Janet W. Díaz, University of North Carolina at Chapel Hill
Gerald Wade, Vanderbilt University

EDITORS

Juan Ramón Jiménez

TWAS 379

Juan Ramón Jiménez

JUAN RAMÓN JIMÉNEZ

By DONALD F. FOGELQUIST
University of California, Los Angeles

TWAYNE PUBLISHERS
A DIVISION OF G. K. HALL & CO., BOSTON

Library of Congress Cataloging in Publication Data

Fogelquist, Donald F.
  Juan Ramón Jiménez.

  (Twayne's world author series; TWAS 379: Spain)
  Bibliography: p. 167-71.
  1. Jiménez, Juan Ramón, 1881-1958.
PQ6619.I4Z615   861'.6'2   75-26547
ISBN 0-8057-6180-2

MANUFACTURED IN THE UNITED STATES OF AMERICA

To Helen

Contents

About the Author

Donald F. Fogelquist received the B.A. and M.A. degrees from Washington State University and the Ph.D. from the University of Wisconsin. He directed the Paraguayan-American Cultural Center in Asunción, Paraguay in 1946-1947. Sponsored by the Cultural Division of the United States State Department, Professor Fogelquist made a lecture tour of Latin America in 1959, and in 1962-1963 he was a Fulbright research scholar in Spain. Professor Fogelquist is the author of *Juan Ramón Jiménez. Obra. Bibliografía; The Literary Collaboration and the Personal Correspondence of Ruben Darío and Juan Ramón Jiménez; Españoles de América y americanos de Espana* and has translated *Lincoln in Martí by Emeterio S. Santovenia.* In addition he has published many articles on Spanish and Spanish-American literature in American, Spanish, and Spanish-American literary journals. Professor Fogelquist met Juan Ramón Jiménez in 1941 and was a close friend of his from that time until Jiménez' death. He has been a member of the faculty of the Department of Spanish and Portuguese of the University of California, Los Angeles, since 1948. He has also been a visiting professor at summer sessions of the University of Puerto Rico, Harvard, the University of Arizona summer school in Guadalajara, Mexico, and the University of New Mexico.

Preface

The poetic production of Juan Ramón Jiménez extends over a period of more than fifty years, from the beginning of the twentieth century until well past the midcentury mark. His first two published volumes of poetry appeared in 1900, his *Third Poetic Anthology,* the last, in 1957. What is exceptional about this long career devoted to poetry is that there is no decline in the poet's creative enthusiasm, nor in his capacity for renovation. He never reached a stage at which his evolution stopped and he was satisfied to rest on his laurels. Jiménez never considered his work finished.

The contemporary Spanish critic Angel Valbuena Prat has stated that Jiménez is the key to the Spanish poetic renovation in which his generation was involved, and which continued through all the succeeding generations, a view generally accepted today by those who know contemporary Spanish literature. To Jiménez renewal meant neither the cult of novelty nor the disparagement of tradition. He was always receptive to the new, but always cognizant also of the values of his own cultural antecedents. As a young man he was a devotee of certain French poets, Romantics and Symbolists, among them Musset, Baudelaire, Verlaine, Samain and Jammes. Their influence is easily discernible in the work of Jiménez' "first period", or, approximately, until the beginning of World War I, to use a convenient chronological guidepost. However, the conscious imitation of French models during this period did not lead Jiménez to reject or belittle his Hispanic poetic legacy. Bécquer was the idol of his formative years, and long after Jiménez' enthusiasm for the French poets waned, his admiration for the Sevillan poet remained undiminished. He saw that Bécquer had restored to Spanish verse some of the intensity and essentiality with which the great mystic poets of the sixteenth century had imbued it, but which since then had been lost. Jiménez was an intermediary in the transmission of the poetic heritage, which Bécquer had rediscovered, to new generations of Spanish poets, but he was also an innovator in his own right.

This study attempts to give an orderly exposition of Jiménez' poetic evolution, showing that he was both a renovative and a stabilizing influence in contemporary Hispanic literature, but always strongly individualistic. I have commented briefly, in chronological order, on individual poetic works or series of works, using representative poems—which I have translated into English—to illustrate various stages of Jiménez' poetic development and the stylistic features of each. I have also supplied what seemed to be the necessary biographical background. An exhaustive and definitive analysis of all of Jiménez' writings and a complete biography would be far too extensive to be contained in a volume like the present one. This study is only intended to be a general survey of the poet's life and works.

Critics have fallen into the habit of dividing Jiménez' work into two periods, considering *Diario de un poeta recién casado* (*The Diary of a Newly Married Poet*) to be the beginning of a new direction in poetry. I have not deviated from this established pattern, but I believe that, like all generalizations, it requires some qualification. In *Estío* (*Summer*), the work which precedes *Diary,* there is already an observable departure—as we shall see presently—from the manner typical of the earlier books. Conversely, while it is true that Jiménez shows a marked preference for free verse in his second period, he reverts from time to time to fixed forms used earlier, particularly the octosyllabic· verse. Thus it becomes apparent, from these and other examples that could be adduced, that the two periods are not so sharply separated as one might suppose. An examination of his total work shows that, despite the changes it undergoes because of changes in the poet's life and in his thinking, there is unity to the whole, a unity which comes from its subjective character rather than from its structure or technique.

However threadbare the word beauty (*belleza*) may have become from centuries of use and abuse, it still has meaning in Jiménez. His devotion to beauty was not so much a reasoned esthetic posture as an ardent religious cult. He saw it in nature, the fountainhead of his imagery, and he came at last to identify it with poetry and with God. It is this sentiment which gives his work its thread of unity, gaining in intensity as the poet advances in age.

Preface

I have commented at some length on Jiménez' relations with Spanish America, partly because of the importance these ties had in his own poetic formation and partly because of the very extensive influence he later exerted in Spanish America. At the beginning of the twentieth century Rubén Darío was the poet of greatest prestige in Spain as well as in Spanish America, a position no previous Latin-American poet had ever attained. Thanks mainly to Darío, Jiménez had an auspicious introduction to the literary world of Madrid. In his letters Jiménez always addressed Darío as "master", clearly recognizing in him a mentor as well as a friend. Darío was also instrumental in making Jiménez known to Spanish-American readers. By 1936, the year Jiménez came to the New World to stay, he was recognized throughout Spanish America as one of the most gifted and influential poets of the Spanish language. He now occupied, in effect, the position which Darío had held a generation earlier.

Although Jiménez lived in the United States longer than in any of the Spanish-speaking countries of the Western Hemisphere, he was much less widely-known here than in Latin America. Relatively few Americans knew that the poet to whom the Nobel Prize was awarded in 1956 had lived in their country for twelve years. Jiménez shunned publicity, but the public incognizance of his life and activity in the United States was mostly attributable to the fact that he wrote exclusively in Spanish. However, in the American academic community he had become known to many students and scholars, among whom he was respected and admired for what he was: a universal poet, whose work was clearly one of the enduring values of Spanish literature.

I am deeply grateful to Francisco Hernandez-Pinzón Jiménez, the poet's nephew, for the kindness and hospitality with which he and his family received me in their home in Madrid, for the numerous books and documents he made available to me, and for his permission to quote the poetry of Juan Ramón Jiménez. To William and Mary Roberts I give my sincerest thanks for permission to quote from their fine translation of *Platero and I*. I am indebted to the many persons whose books and articles I consulted in the preparation of this study.

DONALD F. FOGELQUIST

The University of California, Los Angeles

Chronology

1881   Juan Ramón Jiménez born in Moguer, province of Huelva, Spain on December 23, 1881.

1885-   (approx.; Attends kindergarten and primary school in
1889   Moguer.

1891   Attends Jesuit school in Puerto de Santa María.

1896   Completes *bachillerato* in June 1896.

1897   Studies painting in Seville. Begins legal studies in Seville but soon abandons them. Returns to Moguer.

1900   Goes to Madrid in April. Meets Ruben Darío, Francisco Villaespesa, Salvador Rueda, Ramón del Valle Inclán and other writers. Returns to Moguer in June. Publishes his first two books of verse, *Almas de violeta* (*Violet Souls*) and *Ninfeas* (*Water Lilies*). Deeply afflicted by the sudden death of his father.

1901   Sent to Sanatorium of Castel d'Andorte in Bordeaux, France to recover from nervous disorder aggravated by the death of his father. Returns to Madrid and enters the Sanatorio del Rosario under the care of Dr. Simarra.

1902   Publishes *Rimas* (*Rhymes*). Meets Antonio and Manuel Machado.

1903   Begins publication of the literary review *Helios*. Publishes *Arias tristes* (*Sad Airs*). Moves from Sanatorio del Rosario to the house of Dr. Simarra.

1904   Publishes *Jardines lejanos* (*Distant Gardens*). Frequents La Institución Libre de Enseñanza.

1905   Visits Guadarrama Mountains. Leaves Dr. Simarra's house and returns to Moguer. Publishes *Pastorales* (*Pastorals*).

1905-   Lives in Moguer. Writes without interruption. Publishes
1912   nine books of poetry.

1912-   Returns to Madrid. Lives at the Residencia de Estudiantes.

1916   Associates there with leading writers and intellectuals of the day: Unamuno, Antonio Machado, Oretga y Gasset and others. Meets Zenobia Camprubí Aymar. In 1914 publishes *Platero y yo* (*Platero and I*). Travels to New York. Marries Zenobia Camprub/ Aymar. Publishes *Diario de un poeta recién casado* (*Diary of a Newly Married Poet*). With Zenobia returns to Madrid.

1916- Juan Ramón and Zenobia live in Madrid. Jiménez publishes
1936   four new volumes of poetry, an anthology, many prose pieces. Involved in literary polemics. In 1936 publishes *Canción* (*Song*), intended to be first volume of complete works.

1936   Civil war Breaks out. Jiménez, accompanied by Zenobia, goes to the United States as a cultural emissary of the Spanish Republic. After a short stay in Washington they go to Puerto Rico.

1936- Live in Puerto Rico and Cuba. Move to Miami in 1939.
1939

1939- Live in Miami. Jiménez lectures at the University of Miami
1942   and Duke University. Publishes *Españoles de tres mundos*
1942- (*Spaniards of Three Worlds*), 1942.
1948   Live in Washington, D. C. and Riverdale, Maryland. Both teach at the University of Maryland. Jiménez publishes *La estación total* (*The Total Season*), 1946; *Romances de Coral*
1948- *Gables* (*Coral Gables Ballads*), 1948.
1951   Invited to Argentina and Uruguay to give series of lectures on poetry. Publishes *Animal de fondo* (*Animal of Depth*), 1949. Return to Riverdale. Jiménez in ill health. He and
1951- Zenobia move to Puerto Rico.
1958   Remain in Puerto Rico. Jiménez lectures at the University of Puerto Rico. Zenobia dies of cancer in 1956. Jiménez receives Nobel Prize for Literature in 1956. Publishes *Tercera antología poética* (*Third Poetic Anthology*), 1957. Final illness. Dies in 1958.

CHAPTER 1

The Birthplace, Childhood and Adolescence of Juan Ramón Jiménez

M OGUER, the birthplace of Juan Ramón Jiménez, is very much like dozens of other towns of Andalusia, the region which embraces Spain's southernmost provinces. Solid rows of one and two story houses, intensely white in the bright sunlight, line the narrow cobbled streets. The black wrought-iron balconies and window bars (*rejas*) stand out like fresh print on a white page. Small shops and stores occupy the same building as the living quarters of the owners. Open doors offer a glimpse of the dark interiors, where a counter and a few shelves display a modest assortment of household articles and foods. Around noon the bakery is a busy place, its customers attracted by the appetizing smell of freshly baked bread which drifts through the open doorway.

The townspeople in their dress, bearing and speech are rural. Men with faces darkened and furrowed by constant exposure to sun and weather amble through the streets. Sharp silhouettes of old women dressed entirely in black move silently against the white walls of the town. The occasional office worker in city attire looks out of place here, just as the sibiliant speech of Castile is a dissonant note in this genuinely Andalusian environment.

Automobiles and trucks occasionally bounce and rattle through the main streets of the town, but the horse and donkey are still present. Rural sounds and smells are in the air everywhere—the clatter of farm carts, the braying of donkeys and the crowing of roosters; the scent of grass, hay and dung.

Moguer lies on low hills and offers a view in all directions of fields of grain; olive, orange, fig and peach orchards; vineyards; and pasture. The higher elevations beyond the immediate area of tilled fields are covered with small pines. Seen from the town, they form a dark fringe where hills meet sky. In the spring wild flowers

17

in astonishing profusion bloom on the hills, in the fields and along the roadways—yellow, white, blue, lavender, pink, purple, red, orange in endless variety.

Viewed from the hills, Moguer is a compact huddle of white buildings with rust-colored tile roofs. The tower of its sixteenth century church, Iglesia de Nuestra Señora de la Granada, rises high above the cluster of houses. Compared sometimes, and not ineptly, to the famous Giralda of Seville, it gives Moguer its only dramatic accent. The church is of impressive dimensions, much larger than one might expect of a town the size of Moguer. The interior is of austere simplicity, but the round arches and the plain gray and tan stone lend it a quality of dignity and strength. The height of the nave is sufficient to create a total effect of grandeur. Stained glass windows, the only suggestion of opulence, soften the light and the severity of the stone. The church has two paintings of note, the "Adoration of the Kings" by Murillo and the "Child Jesus" by Alonso Cano, but in the dim light of the chapel where they hang their detail is indistinct.

The other important religious and artistic monument of Moguer is the Convent of Santa Clara, founded in the fourteenth century, a long and rather low church-convent built of brick in Gothic *mudéjar* style, reflecting the strong Moorish influence observable everywhere in Andalusia. Once rich in painting, carved wood, tile work and sumptuous ornaments, gifts of Queen Isabel, the convent has suffered the ravages of two wars, the Napoleonic invasion (1808-1814) and the civil war of 1936-1939. Many of its former treasures of art were damaged, destroyed or carried away, but it still retains some of its old character and charm. The alabaster sepulchers of the Portocarrero family remain intact. Some of the intricate *mudéjar* wood carving, damaged by the "communists" during the civil war, has been partially restored. Church and convent are still in use.

Near Moguer the red brackish waters of the Río Tinto flow sluggishly toward the Gulf of Cádiz and the Atlantic Ocean. Moguer, although not a seaport, lies only a few kilometers from the ocean, and its seafarers have given the town its greatest claim to historic distinction. Several men from Moguer were with Columbus on his first voyage to America. The three caravels sailed from the port of Palos de la Frontera—known also as Palos de Moguer—down the Río Tinto and out to the open sea. In a small room of the monastery of La Rábida, a few miles downstream, Columbus and his counselors had conceived the plans for the expedition. There also Columbus worshipped before his journey and after his return. Many centuries earlier Phoenicians and Romans had explored and colonized the region.

The poet's father, Victor Jiménez y Jiménez, was not a native of Andalusia but had come from Logroño province in north-central Spain, attracted—as were also some other members of the family—by the economic possibilities of the productive agricultural region surrounding Moguer. Victor Jiménez, a fair, blue-eyed man of quiet manner and distinguished bearing, loved nature and preferred country to city living. He prospered in Moguer. His extensive vineyards and numerous wineries afforded the family a good living.[1] Juan Ramón, the youngest of his children, was never denied anything in the way of comfort, security and material advantages during his childhood and youth. Some attitudes which the poet displayed in later life are attributable to these circumstances. He was deeply attached to his father, and in temperament resembled him.

His mother, Purificación Mantecón y López Parejo, was Andalusian by birth and ancestry. From comments scattered through the writings of the poet, it is evident that she was a very good mother, although probably more indulgent toward her youngest child than was beneficial for him. Her affection, diligence, patience and fortitude explain in large part his deep attachment to his home and, after childhood, his resort to its shelter and tranquility, particularly in times of stress, boredom and fatigue.

There were four children in the family: Ignacia, the child of Victor Jiménez' first marriage; and Victoria, Eustaquio and Juan Ramón, born to Purificación Mantecón y López Parejo.

The Jiménez family lived in a comfortable two story house on one of the principal streets of Moguer. Formerly called Calle Nueva (New Street), it has been officially renamed to honor the poet, and it is now known as Juan Ramón Jiménez Street. In earlier times it had had other names. The poet was born in another house, which his father had built on Ribera Street overlooking the Río Tinto, but when Juan Ramón was barely six the family moved to the house on Calle Nueva and the latter is the one most intimately associated with his memories of childhood and youth. Fittingly, it is now a museum which contains furniture, books, magazines, paintings and many personal possessions of the poet and his wife. Less appropriately, his earlier home has long served as quarters for the local contingent of *guardias civiles,* those custodians of public order seen everywhere in rural and urban Spain.

The early years of the poet's life were tranquil and happy, as happy as those of any sensitive child could be. The spacious patio around which the house was built was a secure and peaceful haven where he could play or daydream unmolested. The sunlight, the flowers, the well with its marble curb all contributed to the enchantment of this little world.

Juan Ramón's room on the second floor opened onto a balcony which ran the full length of the house on the side facing the street. From this vantage point he could observe the life of the town without being disturbed by its activity or its curiosity. A steep little flight of stairs in a dark passageway led from the second floor to the *azotea,* a roof terrace, surrounded by a low parapet. This was his favorite spot in the house. Here he could see the whole town and the countryside for miles around. At night he often climbed to the *azotea* to watch the moon and the stars.

He learned to ride, and often sought the peaceful solitude of country roads and pine woods on horseback or mounted on a donkey. A small stable adjoined the house on the side away from the street. Through the back door of the house, he could reach the stable and gain the fields without being observed or stopped by curious townspeople.

Very early in life he developed an unusual responsiveness to nature. The light and the dark; the change of seasons; blue or cloudy sky; wind, water, sun and shadow; trees, flowers, birds; the gamut of sounds and colors in nature were part of his daily experience and enjoyment as a child and his sensitivity to them never lost any of its acuteness, even in old age. Nature was, in effect, the sustaining force of his poetic creation and compensated, in a sense, for whatever Moguer lacked in the way of artistic and intellectual stimulation. There is nothing to indicate that it was more than an average town, where there was much more interest in neighborhood gossip and the humdrum details of daily living than in literature or the arts. The Philistines and yokels most certainly outnumbered the citizens who read good books and listened to good music for enjoyment. Despite his fondness for his native town, the poet sometimes complained of its cultural limitations.[2]

A year of kindergarten and three or four years of elementary school were all the formal education Jiménez received in Moguer. Nothing of consequence has been recorded about these years, nor did Jiménez himself appear to have retained any vivid memories of this early schooling. When he was eleven, he and his brother Eustaquio were sent to the Jesuit school, San Luis Gonzaga, in Puerto de Santa María, near Cádiz. Here, at the age of fifteen, he completed his secondary studies.

The instruction he received at the Jesuit secondary school (*colegio*) was probably as good as any available in the region. The records show that Juan Ramón was a good student and that his behavior was orderly and respectful. However, he was not happy, partly because he did not enjoy the confinement and the discipline of the school. Later in life he spoke with more more detachment than sentimentality about the years spent there.[3] What helped him dominate his homesickness and his aversion to regimentation was his interest in some of the subjects he was required to take. He was alert, imaginative, curious about the world in which he lived, and he did well in such varied subjects as geography, Latin, French, rhetoric and mathematics.[4] Drawing and literature appealed to him strongly. His meditative turn of mind, his love of nature and his intense yearning to catch a glimpse of what lay beyond it impelled him quite naturally toward religion. He was essentially religious and remained so all his life, even though in his maturity he was wont to speak disparagingy of anything that savored of dogma and he sometimes inveighed against Catholicism. Among the six books of his student days which he kept permanently were *The Bible* and the Spanish translation of Thomas a Kempis' *Imitation of Christ*.[5]

After attaining the *bachillerato* at Puerto de Santa Maria, Jiménez went to Moguer for a brief visit with him family, then to Seville to study painting. The choice was his own, although it was his father's intention that he should study law at the University of Seville. A number of paintings from his days in Seville show that Jiménez was a gifted beginner, and that if he had chosen painting as a career he could have become an accomplished artist.

Meanwhile, a passion for poetry had been noticeably stimulated in Jiménez. He read avidly such Romantics as Lamartine, Byron, Espronceda, Heine, Bécquer, Rosalía de Castro. The latter two in particular made a deep and lasting impression on him, a fact he stressed insistently in later years, freely acknowledging his debt to both. He published his first poems in newspapers and magazines of Seville and smaller towns of the province, and soon won local fame. One newspaper published a picture of the young poet and a laudatory article on his work. The early success of his poems was, without doubt, the decisive factor in his choice of poetry over art as a career. The prosperity of his father's vineyards and wine cellars made possible this choice betwen two notoriously nonlucrative vocations. The prelaw studies which Jiménez had begun in Seville had not gone well, mainly because he had neglected his studies to have time for reading his favorite poets and for writing verse. A failure in one of his courses prompted him to give up a career in which he had never had the slightest interest. Jiménez returned to Moguer, not the painter he had hoped to be, nor the lawyer his father had intended him to be, but an incipient poet with a tremendous enthusiasm for his art. However, the few of his early poems that have been preserved give no real indication of what his mature work was to be. They are diffuse, sentimental, charged with the exaggerated romanticism one might have expected of a sixteen or seventeen year old boy of his time and his temperament.

Jiménez returned to Moguer in ill health,[6] occasioned by the fatigue and emotional strain of his experiences in Seville. Although for a time he was under the care of doctors, the creative urge that had seized him in Seville did not abate. He began to send poems to magazines in Madrid and thus to make contacts with writers in the capital. His correspondence with some of them prepared the way for his definitive career as a writer.

Life in Moguer continued its usual uneventful course. During his years at the Jesuit school Jiménez spent vacations in Moguer, and after his return from Seville he resumed his normal place in the family. However, the social activity of the town did not appeal to him, and he consistently avoided large gatherings, hilarity and noise. There were at least two love affairs during adolescence and early manhood, but aside from inspiring some romantic verse they did not visibly affect the course of his life.

The most revealing personal sketch of Jiménez as a boy was one he himself wrote during middle age, in which he spoke of his own willfulness and caprice with unusual candor. The following translated passages are excerpts from the sketch:

As a boy, between thirteen and fifteen years of age, I was violent, terrible, bad. Shotguns fascinated me. I had quite a number of them, ranging from fancy pieces for buck shot to double-barreled guns for bullets, through a considerable variety of models. I was a hunter of everything that was huntable, and my shotgun did a great deal of damage in the surrounding country. I killed, for the sake of killing, sparrows, blackbirds, finches, titmice, doves, crows, hens, cats....Through recklessness, I was on the point of killing other people and myself. I recall that my cousin Ignacio Ríos, younger than I, had an eaglet [7] and he carried it with him everywhere. He came with it to see us at Montemayor and I decided to kill it. He ran like mad, clutching it by the tips of the wings, and I, running after him, fired a shot into the ground. Finally, my poor cousin, not knowing what to do, threw it into the big pond. And there I killed it....

I had to have everything on the dot and just as I wanted it. If not, I got excited, I raged and threatened. Whatever I said had to be done. My mother suffered a great deal during those years because of me....I argued about everything with my aunts and uncles, fifty or sixty years old, and they had to give in to me. The arguments about art, literature, travel were endless and stupid on my part. All these affairs ended with my mother in tears, which exasperated me still more.... [8]

This self-portrait shows a facet of Jiménez' personality which is probably unknown to many of his readers. He could be capricious and unreasonable, and often was, both as a boy and as a man. However, one cannot conclude that his was typical behavior. The letters he later wrote to his mother show him to be an affectionate and considerate son. The fascination of firearms he soon outgrew. His love of birds and animals is well known. Anyone who knew him as an adult would have found it hard to believe that he had ever been capable of killing living creatures and cannonading the countryside with shotgun blasts. He himself admitted that he sometimes had fits of temper, but the very admission is to his credit, as is the repentance which usually followed these outbursts.

CHAPTER 2

Tradition and Change

I *Spain on the Eve of Literary Resurgence*

A deceptive aura of peace and stability had settled over
Spain during the last quarter of the nineteenth century. It was
a relaxed and comfortable period, at least for those who enjoyed
some measure of prosperity and security. Most Spaniards were
satisfied to keep things as they were, and saw no reason to agitate
that "comfortable and deceptive backwater of Spanish life", as
Pedro Laín Entralgo has appropriately called the period.
Politicians of the time were more concerned with keeping up ap-
pearances than with introducing necessary social, economic and
political reforms. There was a flowering both of oratory and
inaction.

The state of Spanish letters was comparable to that of the society
of the day. The most significant novelists, Galdós, Pereda and
Pardo Bazán, followed the realistic and naturalistic trends of
Western Europe. The two leading critics, Juan Valera and
Leopoldo Alas, better known as Clarín, were more traditionalist
than revolutionary in their views, particularly Valera, the older of
the two. Galdós and Pardo Bazán lived through the first two
decades of the twentieth century, but their major works, their
prestige and influence identified them with the preceding century.
Both Valera and Clarín died in 1905. Echegaray, the most
renowned of the dramatists, wrote most of his plays in the seventies
and eighties.[1] The three poets who had reigned unchallenged for
many years were nearing the end of their lives: Zorilla died in 1893,
Campoamor in 1901 and Núñez de Arce in 1903.

In 1891, the third centenary of the death of San Juan de la Cruz,
the Spanish Academy offered a prize of one thousand *pesetas* for
the best poem of mystic inspiration, which elicited from Clarín a
derisive comment on the young poets of the day, whom he styled
"our fin de siécle bards, our Symbolists, our decadents, our in-

24

strumentalists, our mystics...''.[2] Clarín, who kept his hand on the literary pulse of his country, observed a new trend but was skeptical, if not contemptuous, of it. The attitude is typical of an older generation which decries the manners, morals and taste of the succeeding generation, but it may also be true that among the poets he ridiculed there were none of real merit. Young Spanish authors undoubtedly had some acquaintance with the contemporary writers of France, but until Rubén Darío appeared on the scene no one discovered how adaptable Spanish poetic language could be to the same type of innovations that had transformed French poetry.

It was Juan Valera who in 1891 introduced Rubén Darío to the Spanish public with a laudatory article on *Azul* (*Blue*), Darío's first major work, published in Santiago, Chile in 1888. In 1892 the Nicaraguan poet paid his first visit to Spain, serving at that time as secretary of the delegation appointed by his government to represent Nicaragua at the celebration of the fourth centenary of the discovery of America. Darío now had occasion to meet personally not only Valera, who had given *Blue* such an auspicious introduction in Spain, but also the other literary celebrities of the day, including Campoamor, Núñez de Arce and Zorrilla, whom he had venerated during his adolescence. Darío's talent was recognized by the Spanish literary elders, but they were not ready to admit him to their inner circle. Menéndez y Pelayo must have expressed the attitude of his generation with some accuracy when he praised Darío's gifts as a poet, but disapproved of his pursuit of innovation and his tendency to imitate French writers. Among the Spanish poets only Salvador Rueda, who was something of an innovator himself, received Darío with warmth and enthusiasm. In Spain the moment had not yet come for the new generation to assert its independence.

The revolt against literary conventions, which eventually came to be known as "Modernism", began earlier in Spanish America than in Spain. This reversal of normal trends was at least in part a consequence of historical developments. The wounds left by the wars of independence had been slow in healing, and until the centenary of 1892, commemorating the discovery of America, little was done officially to renew the ties between Spain and her former colonies. France tended more and more to replace Spain in the affections and literary preferences of many Spanish Americans during the new era of political independence from Spain. In

America there were no longer viceroys, colonial governors, nor a Royal Spanish Academy of the language to restrain the libertarian impulses of the young. By exception, one Spanish poet attained unusual prestige and influence among the new poets of America. Bécquer, who was ignored or treated with condescension by his contemporaries in Spain, was widely read and imitated in the New World. Darío, Nájera, Casal, Silva, Nervo and many others were indebted to the Sevillan poet.[3] Bécquer was a more subtle and intense poet than any of his Romantic contemporaries in Spain. Rather than a belated Romantic, as some critics have classified him, he could more appropriately be called a forerunner of Symbolism.[4]

The young Spanish American poets of the eighties and nineties were isolated geographically and had little contact with one another, but there was remarkable similarity in their aspirations. Nearly all were dissatisfied with the pomp, prolixity and vapidity of the poetry their fathers read, wrote and declaimed. Most of them looked for deliverance from abroad. Victor Hugo was the first idol of many, but it was the serenity, the refinement, the plastic beauty of the Parnassian poets, and the music, the subtle nuances, the emotional intensity of the Symbolists which revealed to them the greatest possibilities for the transformation of Hispanic poetry. However, the influences were not exclusively French, but came from other European sources as well, and to some extent from the United States, particularly from Poe and Whitman.

The literary climate was more favorable, then, in Spanish America than in Spain for the appearance of a work like Darío's *Blue*, which brought the diversity of new literary tendencies to a focus. Its success was immediate. Although it was not a manifesto of Modernism, its effect on its generation of Spanish Americans might be compared to that of Hugo's preface to *Cromwell* on nascent French Romanticism.

Rubén Darío's contemporaries in Spanish America soon came to regard him as the leader of a new literary movement. By the time he was sixteen he was already something of a poetic celebrity in Central America. At nineteen he traveled to Chile, where his books *Rimas* (*Rhymes*), *Abrojos* (*Thistles*), and *Blue* were published. In 1892, then twenty-five, he hade his first trip to Spain. Not long afterward he journeyed to New York, thence to Paris, and finally to Buenos Aires, where he remained from 1893 to 1898. In Buenos

Aires Darío was surrounded by the leading young intellectuals and writers then living in that city. With the prestige of *Blue* and his cosmopolitan experience behind him, the time was propitious for Darío to exercise his leadership. In collaboration with other young writers he began the publication of *Revista de América,* a literary review which, in spite of its short life, proved to be an important means of circulating the new Modernist tenets and of uniting the new generation against its adversaries.

Prosas profanas, which Darío published in 1896, was received with great enthusiasm by his friends and partisans, and it provoked the indignation of the more conservative element among critics and the reading public. In this volume Darío introduced all the poetic discoveries he had made in recent years. He demonstrated that music and subtlety could be achieved by using new verse forms, reviving old ones, changing the distribution of accents and by defying the conventions that had made for rigidity and monotony in Spanish poetry. He acknowledged his indebtedness to Verlaine but admitted that he drew from many other sources, new and old, particularly Spanish classic writers: Santa Teresa, Quevedo, Góngora, Gracián. The atmosphere of *Prosas profanas* (*Profane Proses*) was one of elegance and aristocracy. Like Góngora, Darío was seeking artistic perfection, not profundity of thought or emotional appeal. *Profane Proses* was a personal triumph for Darío, but more than that it was the vindication of the poetic ideals of the new generation of Spanish-American writers.

Late in 1898 Darío—long a correspondent for the renowned Argentinian newspaper *La nación*—was sent on a special mission to Spain, where he was to observe and report on the conditions that prevailed there after the war with the United States. The debacle that shocked the younger generation of Spanish intellectuals into painful awareness of the national apathy and an examination of the national conscience had its repercussions in Spanish America. For the first time since independence, there was a spirit of solidarity among all the Spanish-speaking countries. Those of the New World felt that Spain's loss of power and prestige was also their loss, and in the expansion of their powerful northern neighbor they saw a new threat to their own security.

Darío arrived in Spain early in 1899. Accustomed as he was to life in Argentina, a young, vigorous and rapidly developing nation, he was disheartened by the atmosphere of resignation and in-

difference he found in Spain. There seemed little concern over the
fact that the nation's statesmen had allowed it to be despoiled of its
last colonies. Political squabbling seemed to have priority over
reconstruction. Darío's appraisal of the state of Spanish letters was
equally pessimistic. He commented that some of the distinguished
figures he had met on his first visit were now dead, that Núñez de
Arce and Campoamor were old and infirm, that Valera was blind.[5]

Darío was soon to discover that his first impressions were
somewhat deceptive, for Spain was on the eve of a remarkable
resurgence. Francisco Giner de los Ríos, a genial educator,
philosopher and humanist, was responsible more than any other
individual for the cultural orientation of the new generation of
Spaniards. The aspiration of the "Generation of 1898" was the
revitalization of every aspect of Spanish life. In June 1898, shortly
after the destruction of the Spanish fleet in the Philippines, a new
Madrid magazine, *Vida Nueza (New Life)*, issued its first number.
It contained an article which expressed the views of many
disillusioned Spaniards, particularly the young.

New life! That is what millions of Spaniards are saying, tired of what is
old, worn, conventional, of what exists nowhere except among us. New
life! That means new vigor in political parties, new vigor in ideas; enough
of routine, of injustice, of the selfishness of the privileged, of the
misfortunes of the oppressed; of exploitation, of outmoded reactionary
thinking. For fifty years Spanish life has always been the same. Everything
is old among us: politics, literature, art, customs, taste, business, industry,
daily life.[6]

The changes which took place in succeeding years were not so
general and profound as many had hoped they would be, but there
was a notable renaissance of Spanish literature. In this literary
revival the two main figures were, at the outset, Miguel de
Unamuno and Rubén Darío. Unamuno was an original thinker, an
iconoclast, a passionate and exalted poet. His dynamic personality,
his unconventionality, his vigorous literary style and the deep
emotional current that ran through his writing left their mark on
nearly all his contemporaries. He sometimes spoke derisively of
Darío and the Modernists but he saw their merits as well as their
defects. His sobriety was an effective counterbalance for Darío's
exuberance. Unamuno's influence deepened and intensified

Spanish poetry; that of Darío gave it new subtlety, beauty and music.

Profane Proses brought a brilliance and refinement to Spanish lyric poetry that it had never known before.[7] Darío became the idol of the new poets of Spain and his prestige soon was as great there as in America. Up to this time literary modes had always passed from Spain to Spanish America; but now they moved in the inverse direction. Darío's poems appeared regularly in the literary magazines of Madrid, he spoke at public gatherings, he had a retinue of admirers with whom he wined, dined and discussed literature and art. Just as he had been in Buenos Aires, Darío was now embroiled in the controversy between the old and the new literary generations of Madrid.

Perhaps there was in Spain no more avid reader of the young Spanish-American poets, nor a more loyal partisan of Rubén Darío, than the young poet Francisco Villaespesa. Together they sought to reform Spanish poetry. It was in *New Life,* the new literary magazine to which both contributed, that they discovered a kindred spirit in Juan Ramón Jiménez. The first poem Jiménez sent to *New Life* elicited such a favorable response that he soon became a regular contributor to the magazine. One day early in the spring of 1900 he came to a decisive moment in his life. That day he received a post card from Villaespesa and Rubén Darío inviting him to come to Madrid to collaborate with them in the reformation of Spanish poetry. Jiménez needed no urging, for he looked on Darío as the Modernist genius and Messiah. He gathered up his poems, packed his bags and set out for Madrid without delay. In Madrid new friends gave him a warm welcome, among them several of the young writers of greatest promise. Villaespesa was for a time his constant companion, and with Darío he formed a friendship which lasted until the Nicaraguan poet's death in 1916.

II *The Early Poetic Works of Juan Ramón Jiménez*

The publication in 1900 of his first two books of verse, *Almas de violeta* (*Violet Souls*) and *Ninfeas* (*Water Lilies*), marked the definitive beginning of Jiménez' career as a poet. From this point on he was to devote himself exclusively to writing. The former of these works was printed in purple ink, the latter in green, a detail for which the irrepressible Villaespesa was responsible. For *Violet Souls* Villaespesa also wrote an effusive introduction, in which he disparaged the "decrepit old men" of the poetic generation in eclipse and exalted the new generation, whose watchword was "art for art's sake". Among the leaders of "the new crusade", was Juan R. Jiménez "a new Lohengrin, guiding the snowy swan toward the remote shores of the enchanted Thule."

The prevailing tone of the eighteen poems of *Violet Souls* is one of melancholy sentimentality. Both the content and the expression are Romantic. Death is the most frequent theme; nostalgic evocation of the past is the second in importance. Only one composition, entitled *"Azul"* (*"Blue"*), the shortest in the collection, is a love poem. There is a monotonous repetition of the adjective *triste* (*sad*) and frequent use of *solo* (*alone*), *frío* (*cold*), *muerto* (*dead*), as well as nouns and verbs of the same character. Exaggerated sentimentality is relieved only occasionally by a note of simple, lyric beauty and sincere emotion. A number of passages are reminiscent of the Spanish-American Modernists, particularly the Colombian poet José Asunción Silva and the Mexican Gutiérrez Nájera. In his versification, following Rubén Darío's example, Jiménez used a variety of forms, some of them quite irregular, but it is apparent even in this volume that he achieved his best effects with the octosyllabic ballad form (*verso de romance*) which was later to become his favorite meter.

Water Lilies is a much longer work than *Violet Souls* but not superior to it in any sense. The poems are contrived, morbid, wordy, superficial. Obviously, Jiménez wrote them at a time when he found the fascination of Modernism irresistible. Several of the compositions follow the rhythmic pattern used so effectively by Silva in his famous "Nocturno" ("Nocturne"), first published in Spain in 1900.[8] A four syllable foot with the stress on the third syllable is used in verses of varying length—four, eight, twelve, sixteen syllables or more—rhymed or unrhymed. With this meter Silva achieved a haunting musical effect which neither Jiménez nor any of the other poets who later used the same form was able to attain.[9]

For *Water Lilies* Rubén Darío wrote a poetic introduction, or "atrio", as he styled it, a sonnet in fourteen syllable (alexandrine) verse, a form which he prided himself on having introduced in the

Spanish-speaking world. Jiménez used the same alexandrine sonnet form for several of his poems and varied the form further by writing "sonnets" of twelve, thirteen and eighteen syllable lines, much as Darío had done in his second edition of *Blue,* published in 1892. Darío's influence is evident also in the sensual imagery of *Water Lilies,* a natural mode of expression in the Nicaraguan poet, but an affectation in his young follower.

The comments of the critics on the two books were an explosion of indignant protest. A few years later, Jiménez himself, referring to the reaction, declared that never had a poet been subjected to such castigation by the "school masters" or the "draymen" of the press.[10] However, Darío himself had fared no better at the hands of the older Spanish critics, who considered him the main culprit in a Modernist plot to sabotage the poetic language of the Spanish-speaking countries. These attacks were completely ineffectual in repressing the enthusiasm that many young writers felt for Darío and the poetic innovations he introduced.

Jiménez' first two books received applause as well as censure. A Sevillan critic, Timoteo Orbe, gave what may have been as accurate a judgment as any then passed on the possibilities of the young Jiménez as a poet. Orbe criticized the affectation and extravagance of the two books, but saw the reason behind them: a commendable desire to emerge from the stagnation into which Spanish poetry had fallen. He considered innovation and renewal a necessity in art, but cautioned Jiménez and the other young poets of the day against abuse of novelty, urging them not to reject the heritage their own classic writers had left them. Orbe was convinced that Jiménez had great poetic talent and that the wisdom and moderation which would come to him with increased age and experience would eliminate from his poetry the verbiage and affectation which at present encumbered it. The prediction proved to be completely accurate.[11]

The opening year of the twentieth century was one of the most eventful in the life of Juan Ramón Jiménez. The trip to Madrid, the acquaintance with Rubén Darío and several other writers, the publication of his first two books, his acceptance by the "new" writers as a member of the inner circle all took place in 1900. However, it was also marked by a personal tragedy which deeply affected the poet. Not long after his return from Madrid, his father died suddenly of a heart attack. The death aggravated Juan

Ramón's nervous illness, the aftermath of the overstimulation experienced in Madrid. An intense, morbid anxiety seized the poet. He became so obsessed with the fear of sudden death that only the presence of a doctor could soothe him, an unpredictable anxiety which was to reappear from time to time in later years.

Taken by his family to a sanatorium in Bordeaux, Jiménez spent the better part of the year 1901 there recuperating from his illness.[12] The experience proved beneficial, not only to his health, but to his literary aspirations as well. In Bordeaux he read extensively, particularly the works of Baudelaire and the Symbolists Mallarmé, Verlaine, Rimbaud. There also he wrote *Rimas* (*Rhymes*), his third book, published in Madrid in 1902.

The title *Rhymes* obviously had been suggested by Bécquer, whose own book *Rimas* (*Rhymes*) Jiménez had read with impassioned interest and practically knew by heart. That Bécquer was the model for the new book is evident both in the form and content. The meter Jiménez used most consistently in this work is the eight syllable verse, either in a four line stanza or stanzas of varying length, unrhymed but employing assonance in the even lines. He also used the hendecasyllable in similar manner, sometimes combining it with a seven syllable verse in a four line stanza with assonance in the even lines, ending usually with an accented syllable. With this type of versification Bécquer had given his poetry a flexibility and freshness which offered a pleasing contrast to the rigid and monotonous patterns used by most of the poets of his time. Although much of the sadness and the morbidity of Jiménez' earlier poems persist in *Rhymes,* they are not dramatized to the extent that they are in *Water Lilies.* The adjectives are more restrained and create a vague, dreamy atmosphere rather than a sensational effect. Words of more subtle suggestion—*pálido* (pale), *vago* (vague), *sereno* (serene), *tranquilo* (tranquil), *lejano* (distant), *inefable* (ineffable), *soñoliento* (sleepy)—tend to replace the emphatically morbid adjectives of *Water Lilies,* such as *funesto* (baneful), *fatal* (fatal), *sangriento* (bloody), *lúgubre* (lugubrious), *nauseabundo* (nauseating), *espantoso* (frightful), *tétrico* (gloomy), *cruento* (cruel), *lascivo* (lascivious), *horrendo* (dreadful).

When he wrote *Rhymes* Jiménez had come to at least a partial realization that indiscriminate reliance on hyperbole was ill-suited to his temperament, if indeed it belonged to poetry at all. He had also discovered that novelty of form had in itself no particular virtue. Silva's "Nocturne", perhaps the most startling formal innovation of the Modernist period, proved to be a singular contribution to Hispanic poetry, not because of its novelty, but because the form was so well adapted to the content, and because the musical quality of the verse enhanced the emotional intensity of the poem. In *Rhymes* Jiménez was experimenting, but with better judgment than in *Water Lilies*. In a few poems he still showed some inclination to imitate the Modernists,[13] but there is a discernible trend toward a style that was his own. In his use of Bécquer as a model, there was probably less imitation than natural affinity. Jiménez was perhaps closer to Bécquer in temperament than to any of the major poets he had admired as an adolescent—Byron, Lamartine, Espronceda, Zorrilla, Núñez de Arce, Campoamor, Heine, Baudelaire—or even Verlaine and Rubén Darío. Jiménez had more to learn from Bécquer's short, intense poems than from those of *Profane Proses,* the most important collection Darío had published up to that time and in which the Nicaraguan achieved his greatest elegance and virtuosity.

Jiménez himself stated, many years later, that *Rhymes* was the beginning of his reaction against extreme Modernism.[14] Some of the verbiage and superficiality of the earlier poems was lost in *Rhymes* but one thing persisted: the sentimentality. It is apparent from the fact that ten poems from *Violet Souls* and *Water Lilies* reappear in *Rhymes* that Jiménez had at this point no intention of renouncing his earlier manner or setting out in a completely new direction.[15] Clearly he was an intensely subjective poet and could not reject or suppress what was, paradoxically, his greatest gift and his greatest weakness. The intimate, introverted character of his poetry never changed in any radical sense, although his style—particularly after his early thirties—gained more and more in essentiality and concision, and his emotion became correspondingly more intellectualized.

It was not the sadness of Jiménez' first two books that detracted from their merit, but their cult of sadness, their dramatization of sorrow. Knowing the sheltered and privileged circumstances in which he lived up to the time these books were published, one is disposed to question the profundity of their sentiment.

In many poems the emotion was undoubtedly sincere, but the constant resort to the outward manifestation of grief—accepted as an esthetic principle—obscured the genuine feeling beneath the surface of the poem. Such effusions, although common enough throughout the nineteenth century, were by the beginning of the new century distinctly outmoded. Nothing could be gained by continuing their use. Jiménez was probably aware of this as he wrote *Rhymes*. Thus, although he knew that by nature he could never be an objective poet, he also had come to understand that in genuine poetry emotion could neither be flaunted nor contrived. Although there are, in *Rhymes,* many lapses into the earlier manner, there is also commendable progress toward a more dignified style and the expression of emotional truth.

According to his own admission, it was nostalgia that impelled Jiménez to return to Madrid at the end of 1901. No explanation has been given for his decision to go to Madrid rather than to his home in Moguer, but it is likely that the death of his father had robbed him of the sense of security that his home had formerly given him. In *Rhymes* there are direct allusions to the death of his father, which must have been on his mind constantly.[16] Under the circumstances, the choice of the Sanatorio del Rosario as a refuge would seem natural.

In the Sanatorio the poet occupied an attractive suite of rooms. He was under the care of competent physicians, and his nurses were diligent and kindly nuns. Although the Sanatorio is now hemmed in by apartment buildings and stores, and its tranquility has been lost forever in urban noise and confusion, at the beginning of the century it stood in almost rural surroundings.[17] Here the poet could commune with nature without discomfort or inconvenience. He could see his friends, or not see them, as he chose. He was attended, protected and pampered by kind and solicitous people. The affluence of his family permitted him to live in these ideal circumstances for two years. He recalled them later with fondness and nostalgia: "In this atmosphere of convent and garden I spent two of the best years of my life. Some romantic love, of a religious sensuality, a monastic peace, smell of incense and flowers, a window on the garden, a terrace with rose bushes for moonlit nights...."[18]

Old and new friends, particularly writers, often visited Jiménez at the Sanatorio. There Villaespesa, Salvador Rueda, Valle Inclán, Martínez Sierra, Viriato Diaz Pérez, the Machado brothers and their sisters, feminine friends or relatives were wont to gather. The poet's retreat thus became both a literary salon and a social center.

Such animation and camaraderie had never filled any two years of his life up to this time, and it is doubtful that any later period duplicated this experience.

The poems written during this period were published in 1903 in a volume entitled *Arias tristes (Sad Airs)*. The book has the novel feature of division into three parts or movements, each with the score of a Schubert *lied* for a prelude. Each is dedicated to a friend of the author. The second has an epigraph by Verlaine, and the third, one by Musset. "Nocturnos", the second part, is preceded by the author's own commentary, in which he characterizes his work as "monotonous, full of moonlight and sadness".[19] He ends with an evocation of Heine, Bécquer, Verlaine and Musset and an entreaty that all kindred spirits weep for those who never weep. A glance at these rather theatrical flourishes may well have prepared readers for more poetic fare like that of *Water Lilies,* but it is immediately apparent, on reading the poems themselves, that *Sad Airs* is the work of a more mature poet. In it Jiménez uses the *romance* verse almost exclusively. There are no awkward experiments to gain novelty. The first impression is one of almost artless simplicity, but it is a simplicity achieved through mastery of form. Probably no poet of the time, nor any since, could equal the versatility of Jiménez in the use of the *romance*. In *Sad Airs* this skill is evident for the first time. The use of enjambement is particularly effective in giving the short verse fluidity and music. The poet's delicate sense of euphony is evident in the choice of words suggestive both in sound and sense. The beauty of an image like the following is enhanced by the music of its pleasing succession of liquid sounds, which, unfortunately are lost in the translation: "...in shadow that the full moon of autumn turns golden" ("...en la penumbra que dora / el plenilunio de otoño").

An atmosphere of vague sadness pervades *Sad Airs,* a quality one critic aptly called the "introversion of the landscape".[20] The sentiment is subdued, not dramatic as in many of the earlier poems. The visual imagery contributes further to the mood. Subdued light, haze-enveloped trees, dreamy, tranquil valleys, placid rivers, wisps of smoke floating over distant houses, hills and fields lost in mist, a red moon, a lonely star create a subtle, melancholy enchantment, one of the most appealing features of these poems. The following passage is typical:

... the soft and still
landscape is fading,
laden with mist and sleep.

... el dulce y quieto
paisaje se va borrando,
cargado de niebla y sueño.

Although the *Sad Airs* was written in Madrid, there is nothing in
these poems that suggests a city environment. Many of them have a
pastoral atmosphere reminiscent of rural Andalusia and, directly or
indirectly, this is probably their source of inspiration. The love
poems, because of the cloying sentimentality that often intrudes in
them, are usually inferior to those which express the poet's rapture,
awe or pensiveness in the presence of the natural world. His intense
response to nature is reflected in his tendency to attribute human
emotion to features of the landscape or to natural phenomena. A
great many examples like the following could be cited: "The valley
has a dream / and a heart" ("El valle tiene un ensueño, / y un
corazón") "...a grievously pale moon" ("...una luna /
dolorosamente pálida"); "the water weeps" ("llora el agua");
"the star ... looks at me dead with grief" ("la estrella ... me mira
muerto de pena").

Although Verlaine's influence, next to Bécquer's and that of
Rosalía de Castro, may be the most sustained in this period of
Jiménez' poetic evolution, that of Heine is visible in a number of
poems; at least there is often a noticeable similarity between the
two poets. Both were intrigued by death and found a certain
morbid appeal in its physical aspects, which they often translated
into a sort of spectral imagery or expressed in adjectives denoting
pallor, lividity, withering. Both were extremely sensitive to nature,
and both were aware of, and consciously drew from, the wealth of
poetry of popular inspiration in their respective countries. Short,
intimate lyrics, employing a simple form close to the popular
ballad, were typical of both.

Despite the parallels which may be drawn between Jiménez and
some other poets, *Sad Airs* comes much closer to being his own
mode of expression than any of his earlier works. The best of these
poems are notable for the intensity of their feeling for nature; for

their delicate and original imagery, created with simple elements but with delicate nuances; for their rhythmic grace and spontaneity; for the subtle elegiac tenderness that pervades them, and dignifies them because it is sincere. Much of the diffuseness and the overemphasis of Jiménez' earlier volumes has been eliminated. The *Sad Airs* are purer, more essential poetry. Lapses into exaggerated sentimentality and monotonous repetition occur here with less frequency than in earlier works.

The response of the critics to *Sad Airs* was immediate and highly favorable. It was not unusual that such close friends of Jiménez as Antonio Machado, Pedro González Blanco and Gregorio Martínez Sierra should have written enthusiastic reviews of the poet's latest book, but praise came also from authors who were not his intimates and with whom he could claim no real esthetic kinship. Francisco Navarro Ledesma—to cite one such example—had distinguished himself for his caustic commentaries on the "new" poets. He had been prone to castigate the Modernists, and he was particularly fond of deflating Rubén Darío. However, he found *Sad Airs* to his liking and did not hesitate to say so. Curiously, Navarro Ledesma and Rubén Darío were finally to agree on one matter, their estimate of *Sad Airs*. Darío wrote what was without doubt the most significant critical article yet to be published on Jiménez. He credited the young Andalusian with being the most intense and original Spanish lyric poet since Bécquer.[21] Darío's words were not lost on his contemporaries of Spanish America. Jiménez soon became known in the Spanish-speaking countries of the New World, and his popularity and influence grew with each succeeding volume he published.

In 1903 Jiménez and a group of the young writers then rising to prominence began the publication of the literary journal *Helios*. Although only eleven issues were published, the magazine exerted an important literary influence. Many of the best Spanish and Spanish-American writers of the time wrote for *Helios,* among them Jiménez himself, Antonio Machado, Benavente, Martínez Sierra (one of the editors), Ramón Pérez de Ayala (also on the editorial staff), Valle Inclán, Eduardo Marquina and, of course, Rubén Darío. The latter had gone to Paris to live, but kept up a lively correspondence with Jiménez and sent poems from time to time for the magazine. Except for foreign works, which were published in translation, only original, unpublished pieces were accepted. *Helios* thus contained the first edition of a surprising number of important poems, articles or stories. Jiménez contributed both prose and poetry, as well as translations.

Unamuno, who had never identified himself with any literary group or tendency, least of all Modernism, was probably the most respected and influential Spanish writer of the period. However, in spite of the Modernist leanings of *Helios,* he was not averse to writing for the magazine. In an article addressed to Antonio Machado he expressed views which many of the young writers of the day must have found disconcerting. In a period when the French decadents appealed strongly to many of the younger Spanish writers, Unamuno, with his penchant for swimming against the current, spoke derisively of these foreign literary idols. He urged his young compatriots to draw from the deeper sources of inspiration which they had probably not yet discovered in their own culture and tradition. Jiménez was, without doubt, one of those who could most benefit by such advice. His infatuation with Verlaine is evident in most of the poems he wrote at the time. In *Helios* he published translations of some of Verlaine's poems, and an enthusiastic article entitled "Paul Verlaine and his Beloved the Moon". That he escaped the fate of becoming simply an imitator of French poets, or a second Villaespesa, may have been partly the work of Unamuno.

In 1903 Jiménez left the Sanatorio del Rosario and went to live in the house of Dr. Luis Simarro, whom he had known ever since the death of his father and under whose care he had spent the two years at the Sanatorio. Dr. Simarra, a practicing physician and also a member of the medical faculty at the University of Madrid, was an intellectual liberal. He had a large personal library and was very active in the cultural life of Madrid. Loneliness and desperation, occasioned by the death of his wife, led him to ask Jiménez and a young biologist, Nicolás Achúcarro, to make their home with him.

Except for brief interruptions—short trips to Moguer and a summer in the Guadarrama Mountains—Jiménez lived in Simarra's house for two years. Encouraged by Simarra, he read widely, and not exclusively works of literature, as had been his tendency up to this point. He gained some knowledge of science and philosophy, particularly that of Nietzsche. He also studied languages, but neither at this time nor later in life did he attain the mastery of English and German with which he has sometimes mistakenly been credited.

Another important consequence of his association with Simarra was his introduction to the Institución Libre de Enseñanza. This educational and cultural center, under its leaders Francisco Giner and Manuel B. Cossío, exerted a profound influence on the cultural life of Spain during the last quarter of the nineteenth century and the early years of the twentieth.[22] It was particularly active in educational reform, but it concerned itself also with the advancement of all branches of culture. Although it was neither unreligious nor antireligious, it stood for the liberalization of religion, which sometimes brought it into conflict with orthodox Catholicism.

Accompanied by Dr. Simarra, Jiménez attended lectures and discussions at the Institución Libre de Enseñanza. The intellectuals who frequented the Institución had been strongly influenced by the thinking of the German, post-Kantian, idealist philosopher Krause and were alluded to—often with some mistrust and disapproval—as "Krausists".[23] Unquestionably, Jiménez absorbed some of the thought of this group and his outlook was changed by it. Up to this point in his life he had deviated little from traditional Catholic belief, but he must now have found in it some incompatibility with his changed views.[24] He maintained in later years that Giner, the leader of the new enlightenment, was a Christian, and that he himself was a Christian, but his Christianity came closer to that professed by Unamuno than to that of the church. It is possible that his acquaintance with Nietzsche's thinking also had an eroding effect on his earlier religious convictions.

During the period of Jiménez' close association with Dr. Simarra he wrote and published two more books of poetry. *Jardines lejanos* (*Distant Gardens*), 1904 and *Pastorales* (*Pastorals*), 1905, often considered as part of a trilogy begun with *Sad Airs*. All three are preceded by the musical notations of well-known compositions by Schubert, Gluck, Mendelssohn and Schumann, which give some idea of Jiménez' musical taste during his early twenties. In each the *romance* verse is used almost exclusively, generally in four-verse stanzas with the odd lines unrhymed and with assonance in the even lines. Occasionally, and particularly in *Distant Gardens,* the pattern is varied with abab rime. However, the differences of the three works are greater than these formal and rather superficial similarities.

There is probably no other work of Jiménez in which the allusions to music are so numerous as in *Distant Gardens* and in which the poet's emotional response to music is so often conveyed by the poem. A few quotations will illustrate the point: "The waltzes of the violins / cloud my eyes with tears" ("los valses de los violines / nublan de llanto los ojos"); "rending piano" ("piano desgarrante"); "the sorrowful music / of some old accordian" ("la musica dolorida / de algun viejo acordeon"); "...It is that piano / which is telling my story... / I don't know what tender plaint there is in its sound. ("...Es ese piano / que esta contando mi historia... / Yo no se que tierno llanto hay en su son..."); "The violins were sobbing / beneath the black grove..." ("Sollozaban los violines / bajo la negra arboleda ..."). The phrasing is sometimes reminiscent of Verlaine or Darío. Jiménez' extreme sensitivity to sound is generally observable in the frequency with which auditory imagery occurs in his work. In *Distant Gardens* he makes sentimental abuse of it. Pianos almost invariably weep, the fountain weeps or sobs, the nightingale weeps, the autumn weeps, the poet himself weeps repeatedly.

The sentimentality of *Sad Airs* is sometimes excessive, but it is a book of greater emotional depth than *Distant Gardens*. In the latter neither love nor nature—the essential emotional source of both works—elicits the intensity of feeling with which they are expressed in some of the poems of *Sad Airs*. *Distant Gardens* is more superficial, more conventionally erotic; its imagery is often markedly sensual. This characteristic distinguishes it generally from Jiménez' early works.

The first part of *Distant Gardens* is dedicated to Heine, for whom Jiménez professed great admiration during this period of his life. Occasional passages suggest Heine's influence, but they lack the flippant irony which often tempered the German poet's sentimentality. Several poems are reminiscent in form and content of the Mexican poet, Francisco A. de Icaza, who had long been living in Madrid, and was highly respected in Spanish literary circles. Although Icaza was better known as critic than poet, he probably exerted a more important poetic influence on some of his contemporaries than is generally known. His best poems were simple in form, concise, elegiac, musical, sincere, qualities which Jiménez admired and which he sought in his own poetry.

Pastorals, written when Jiménez was twenty-four, is unique among the poet's early books and stands apart from his poetic works in general. The intense introversion, the persistent sadness, the morbidity which are the mark of his poetry up to 1912 or 1913 intrude less in *Pastorals*. A long stay in the Guadarrama Mountains furnished the motivation for this work, according to Jiménez' own account. The experience drew the poet out of his self-absorption and fixed his attention on this new world of grandeur, solitude and mystery. This was quite different from watching the moon from a window of the sanatorium or from meditation on nature as he observed it from a balcony overlooking a garden or a park. The effect was salubrious. In *Pastorals* the poet is not so much the center of the world as a fascinated observer of its marvels. In these poems he is closer to Francis Jammes than to Verlaine. His emotion is directed outward as much as inward. Often he expresses his delight in nature. The opening stanzas of two poems exemplify the mood:

> The sun will brighten the leaves,
> give diamonds to the river,
> sing songs of gold and laughter,
> with the wind amid the pines ...

> El sol dorará las hojas,
> dará diamantes al río,
> hará un canto de oro y risa,
> con el viento por los pinos ...

> (PLP, 619)

> the sky was full of enchantment
> above the green of the pines ...
> The wind fled, the water, the frog
> and the cricket were singing ...

> El cielo andaba de encantos
> sobre el verdor de los pinos ...
> Huía el viento, cantaban
> el agua, el sapo y el grillo ...

> (PLP, 663)

The *Romancero,* that treasure of popular Spanish ballads whose origins are lost in the past, was one of the traditional sources from which Jiménez most often drew his inspiration.[25] The poems of *Pastorals* have the deceptive simplicity, the ingenuousness and the profundity of some of the traditional *romances*. Jiménez enriched the *romance* with fantasy and music. Emotion is more restrained in *Pastorals* than in any of his earlier works, but it is also more mature and universal. In *Pastorals* Jiménez demonstrated his remarkable faculty for poetic renovation achieved through traditional form. His *romances* are infused with a new magic, not inherent in the form itself, but a product of his own sensibility.

CHAPTER 3

The Moguer Years

SINCE the sixteenth century Madrid has been both the literary and the political center of Spanish life. Spaniards with literary aspirations have inevitably been drawn to Madrid, and those who have won recognition as writers have normally made their permanent residence there. Miguel de Unamuno, who rarely conformed to established patterns, was a notable exception. Unamuno spent the best years of his maturity in the provincial university city of Salamanca, whose environment he found much more peaceful and in tune with his temperament than that of Madrid. Repelled by the city's sordidness and confusion, he spoke disparagingly of Madrid. Antonio Machado also avoided Madrid, preferring life in Soria, Segovia and Baeza, smaller cities where the countryside which he loved was always easily accessible.

Like these two countrymen of his, whom he admired, Jiménez was attracted more by rural and provincial Spain than by its capital.[1] Late in 1905 illness and nostalgia caused him to return to his home again. This time he was to remain in Moguer for an unbroken period of six years. His mother, brother, sisters and other relatives still remained in the town. There he was able to rest and to resume his writing.

A kilometer or two from Moguer on the pine-covered hills that overlook the town, the Jiménez family owned a country retreat called Fuentepiña where the poet spent much of his time. The house, a white one story building with tile roof and an arcaded verandah, was surrounded by a flower garden. It was secluded, but on every side afforded a view of grassy meadows, pine woods, groves of eucalyptus and poplars. A large pine, with the spreading limbs and round crown peculiar to the common Spanish species, cast its shadow over a large area at one corner of the house. This pine, which is still standing, delighted Jiménez, and he mentions it

often in his writings. Many years after he left Moguer nostalgia
possessed him whenever he saw a pine tree. The pine appears in his
poetic imagery from his earliest to his latest period, somewhat
analagous to the birch in the poetry of Robert Frost or the live oak
in that of Antonio Machado.

I   *Baladas de Primavera* (Ballads of Spring)

During the Moguer years Jiménez wrote assiduously. Many of
the poems must have been composed at Fuentepiña, where nature
was both a refuge from the discord and cacophony of urban life,
and a profound source of creative inspiration. The poems of these
years center on nature and love. Although the elegiac tone still
prevails, there is in some poems a new note of jubilation, particularly in *Baladas de primavera* (*Ballads of spring*), a collection
written in 1907 but not published until 1910. These poems are a
joyous song of spring, the expression of the poet's delight in
nature, and at times in a pagan love reminiscent of Rubén Darío. In
them Jiménez used a variety of pleasing metrical innovations,
somewhat as Rubén Darío had done in his *Profane Proses*.

In 1936, referring to his early books, Jiménez spoke of *Rhymes*
as the beginning of his reaction against Modernism (see Chapter 2,
p. 33). What he meant by this statement was certainly not that at
that point in his poetic evolution he repudiated Modernism[2] and
turned his back on Rubén Darío, its high priest.[3] Much of the
confusion that has always obscured·questions related to Modernism arises from the disparity of views as to what it really was.
Jiménez' own opinions on the subject have not served notably to
dissipate the fog generated by poets, journalists and scholars, who
have bickered endlessly and often acrimoniously concerning the
movement, its origins and its characteristics.[4] However, one trend
of Modernism is easily discernible and consequently not open to
controversy. All the Modernists were, in varying degrees, ex-
perimenters with form. In this respect, Modernism persisted in
Jiménez several years beyond the date which is said to have marked
the end of its vogue in Spain.[5] In effect, the Moguer years represent
a return to Modernism after a period in which he used the
traditional *romance* form almost exclusively.

The formal experiments of *Hojas verdes* (*Green Leaves*), the first book written after the return to Moguer, are what most sharply differentiate it from the three works which immediately precede it. Poems written in lines of five, six, eight, nine, ten, eleven, twelve, fourteen syllables, in different combinations and with varying rhyme schemes are proof of the reawakened preoccupation with form. Some of the experiments, particularly the use of syllabic rhyme, suggest that during this period Jiménez may have been as intrigued by technical legerdemain as he was when he wrote *Water Lilies*. The following stanza from the poem *Otra balada a la luna* ("Another Ballad to the Moon") is a good example of the use of this device:

> Tu, que entre la noche bruna,
> en una torre amari-
> lla, eras como un punto, ¡oh, luna!
> sobre una i ... [6]

(PLP, 719)

The brief introduction which Jiménez wrote for *Ballads of Spring* begins with this significant statement: "These ballads are somewhat superficial (exterior); they have more music of the lips than of the soul ...." What is most significant about the comment is its similarity to what critics have written about *Profane Proses,* Darío's work of greatest technical virtuosity. [7] It appears that Jiménez intended to emulate, though not necessarily imitate, Darío in this work. At this moment he too was fascinated by the music of words and may have thought the musical possibilities of the *romance* verse too limited. Another statement in the introduction also reveals that his kinship to the Darío of *Profane Proses* may have been closer than is generally recognized: "...where the flesh appears, the inner flower closes ...", a way of saying that to sing of carnal love is to silence the voice of spiritual aspiration. No doubt his own experience had led him to this conclusion.

The profoundest difference between the two poets may be that while sensuality and eroticism pervade the entire body of Rubén Darío's poetic works, they are present in those of Jiménez for only a relatively brief period, mainly during the six years at Moguer, between 1906 and 1912. In both poets, carnal love often undergoes a poetic sublimation and becomes an element of beauty in the poem. Pedro Salinas has referred to this feature of Darío's poetry as "salvation through the beautiful" ("la salvación por lo bello").[8] The final poem of *Ballads of Spring* illustrates this aspect of the work, and is also typical of the collection as a whole. The first and last stanzas are quoted below:

> Blanca, in the meadow pink with verbena,
> Let me hear your joyful heart;
> God wears blue, life is serene,
> Everything laughs with enchantment and light.
>
> . . . .
>
> Now, that you've come nude like a lily,
> White, naked, radiant with illusion
> Blanca, in the meadow pink with verbena
> Let me hear your joyful heart;
>
> Blanca, en el prado que rosa la verbena,
> déjame oír tu alegre corazón;
> Dios está azul, la vida está serena
> Todo se rie de luz y de illusión.
>
> . . . .
>
> Hoy, que has venido desnuda de azucena,
> blanca, desnuda, radiante de ilusión,
> !Blanca, en el prado que rosa la verbena,
> déjame oír tu alegre corazón!

                         (PLP, 783-784)

There is a happy pantheism here which has its source in the euphoria of love which the poet experiences in the presence of nature. It may have little or nothing to do with the pantheism about which he had no doubt heard his Krausist friends speak at the Institución Libre de Enseñanza. The poem is one of joyous sensuality. No profound spiritual dilemma has yet disturbed Jiménez, at least none comes to the surface in *Ballads of Spring*. The work may also be compared to Darío's *Profane Proses* in this respect. Their song comes more from the lips than from the soul, to paraphrase Jiménez' own statement.

During this period the adjective *azul* (blue) is most often used by Jiménez with the idealized, subjective connotations which the Modernists gave to the word, not simply for its chromatic values. Thus when he says "The afternoon is blue", "blue now envelops life", "God wears blue", his intention is to create an atmosphere of enchantment and mystery which is not implicit in the word blue in normal usage.

The nymphs, satyrs, centaurs and other mythological fauna which appealed so strongly to the Darío of *Profane Proses* appear nowhere in the poetry of Jiménez. There was for him no such thing as vicarious poetic experience. He drew little or nothing from the French Parnassian poets, as the Modernists generally did. The poem was always the product of his own emotional experience. He found little appeal in the exotic trappings that Darío and other Modernists were wont to use as poetic decor. Greek and Germanic mythology, Oriental art and the courtly splendor of eighteenth-century Versailles were never a motif of his compositions nor the source of any of his images or metaphors. They were simply not a part of his poetic universe. He was, of course, indebted to foreign authors, particularly the French. However, his relationship to them was more a matter of personal affinity than literary imitation. He was closer in spirit to Musset than to Vigny, to Verlaine than to Mallarme. His fondness for Samain and Jammes is easy to understand. Tenderness, simplicity, profound love of nature and solitude were attributes of his temperament as well as of theirs.

The rather ephemeral character of Modernism in Spain, as compared to its longevity in Spanish America, may be due in large part to the persistence in Spain of popular poetry as a literary influence. Of the leading Spanish-American Modernists, Jose Martí was probably the only one who was fully aware of the value of this poetic heritage. In Spain it was in the consciousness and the subconsciousness of every poet. The *Ballads of Spring* are technically sophisticated and have some of the virtuosity of *Profane Proses* but the poems have a markedly popular spirit. One of their characteristic features is the use of a rhythmic line as a musical refrain repeated several times in a poem, much like a popular jingle which has an appealing lilt but conveys no precise meaning. Sometimes ingenuousness and simplicity of expression belie the profundity or the poignancy of the thought, a quality not uncommon in proverbs of popular origin.

II   *The* Elegies

The trilogy of *Elegies*—*Elegías puras* (*Pure Elegies*), *Elegías intermedias* (*Intermediate Elegies*) and *Elegías lamentables* (*Plaintive Elegies*)—written in 1908 but published as separate volumes in 1908, 1909 and 1910 respectively, mark a return to the melancholy and decadent spirit of some of Jiménez' earlier works. The *Elegies* have little of the freshness and charm of *Pastorals* and *Ballads of Spring*. Written entirely in fourteen syllable (alexandrine) verse, they lack the musical quality and the grace of the two other works. The spontaneity is lost in the effort to adapt the content to the form. There is a wordiness that Jiménez might have avoided had he used the *romance* verse. The alexandrine was not the poetic medium that suited him best.

Death again becomes an obsession with the poet, and his imagery becomes lugubrious. Its morbid romanticism is reminiscent of the poems of an earlier day, those of *Water Lilies* or *Rhymes*: "a dolorous charm of sepulchral flesh", "rotten heart", "cursed flesh", "rotten flesh", "black wound", etc. Even the nightingale (ruiseñor negro") suffers a sinister transfiguration. The other distinguishing characteristic of the *Elegies* is their eroticism, more accentuated and Baudelairean than the wholesome eroticism of the *Ballads of Spring*. A remorseful disillusionment with carnal love manifests itself repeatedly in these poems. The opening lines of one composition offer a good example:

> Oh, crystal of my soul! Former purity! Was
> slime what love spun for me with its distaffs?

> Ay, cristal de mi alma! ¡Pureza antigua! ¿Lodo
> era lo que el amor mc hilaba con sus ruecas?

(PLP, 840)

Although there may be excessive dramatization of the erotic theme, there is no reason to doubt that the conflict between flesh and spirit was real. Jiménez always a fundamentally sincere poet, had little capacity for feigning emotion that he did not feel. In the *Elegies* it is evident that he was both attracted and repelled by sex. This dichotomy produced many of the poems of the series. To cite one of many possible examples, there is a poem which opens with this salute to carnal love: "Sensuality, blue poison, how you embellish / dreams with stars ..." ("Sensualidad, veneno azul, como embelleces los sueños con estrellas ..."). However, in the second stanza the poet curses the siren who stands between him and eternal things, and whose "white arms" and "mad legs" stifle the notes of his "sad, pure lyre".

Another poem opens with the imprecation "Woman, abyss in flower, a curse on you ..." The second stanza, quoted below, summarizes the content of the poem:

> I went along singing one day, through the golden meadow,
> God touched the world with blue and I was gay and strong;
> You were in the meadow, you opened for me your treasure,
> I fell among your roses and I fell to my death!

> Yo iba cantando un día, por la pradera de oro,
> Dios azulaba el mundo y yo era alegre y fuerte;
> tú estabas en la hierba, me abriste tu tesoro,
> ¡y yo caí en tus rosas y yo caí en la muerte!

(PLP, 896)

Misogyny is far from being a common theme or sentiment in the poetry of Jiménez, but it appears in a number of poems of the elegies. That it did not elicit the best metaphors of which the poet was capable is quite apparent in the quotations given above. However, these should not be considered typical of his work as a whole.

In the *Elegies* Jiménez also introduces touches of realism and irony. Toward the end of the third volume of the series—*Plaintive Elegies*—there is a poem in which he interrupts his lyric meditation to protest against the objectionable habits of men whose society he would happily avoid. The first stanza is quoted below:

In melancholy sun—oh ennui vespertine!—
There floats the bluish fog, the idle exhalation
Of men who smoke, who talk, and drink their wine,
Who grieve the soul and are the mind's vexation.

En el sol meláncolico— oh tedio vespertino!—
flota el humo azulado que exhala la pereza
de estos hombres que fuman, que hablan, que beben vino,
que dan dolor de alma y dolor de cabeza.

(PLP, 892)

It is evident that the poet's aversion to conventional social activity, which was at a later date to be the subject of so much criticism and gossip, by the age of twenty-seven had become an ingrained trait of his personality. The *Elegies,* in effect, end on this note. The final poem derides the outward display, pretense and pompousness of men the poet sees around him: "justices of peace, expert agriculturists, doctors"—the elite of Moguer, no doubt. He, "humble nightingale of the countryside", was silent before them.

Jiménez, like his fellow Andalusian Góngora, could wield satire with dexterity, but his natural bent was for lyric, not satiric, expression. Even his most unimpressive works are redeemed by passages of haunting lyricism. Whatever the defects of the *Elegies* may be, these poems contain many subtle and moving passages, much lyric beauty. The critics of the day commented very favorably on these volumes, crediting Jiménez with the ability to capture elusive emotional nuances with a sureness and delicacy that no other Spanish-speaking poet possessed.

III   *Further Biographical Notes*

If Jiménez observed society with some distaste and disillusionment, it was not because he had been denied recognition in the literary world. Ever since 1900 when Darío had welcomed him to Madrid, he had had a reputation that most young writers would have envied. In Spanish America, as well as Spain, he had his admirers and followers. In 1904 a group of young Peruvian writers, anxious to establish contacts with Jiménez and to obtain his books, resorted to the stratagem of writing letters to him under the name of Georgina Hübner, a girl of Lima and a relative of one of the writers. The scheme proved more successful than its authors had anticipated, and Jiménez, taken in completely by the ruse, became more deeply infatuated with the girl with each exchange of letters. Finally, determined to go to Lima to declare his passion in person, he dispatched an amorous letter to Georgina—or more accurately to those who were using her name—announcing that he was leaving for Peru on the first boat and would soon be by her side. On receipt of Jiménez' letter, the conspirators, seeing that they must act quickly, cabled the Peruvian consul in Madrid—who was innocent of the trick—that Georgina Hübner had died, and asked him to convey the news to Juan Ramón Jiménez, with their condolences.

The "death" of Georgina Hübner inspired a poem that is better known throughout the Spanish-speaking world than scores of much better compositions by Jiménez. The story has been the subject of more articles and commentaries than its scant importance—anecdotal rather than literary—could possibly justify. Under the title "Carta a Georgina Hübner" ("Letter to Georgina Hübner") en el cielo de Lima" the poem was published in the collection *Labertino* (*Labyrinth*), about which more will presently be said.

In 1910, when Jiménez was only twenty-eight, he was elected to membership in the Royal Spanish Academy, the highest recognition Spain confers on its men of letters. The honor rarely comes to an author as young as Jiménez then was, and it would certainly have been cause for elation to almost any writer except him. However, he declined the membership, not only in 1910 but also on two later occasions, once during the days of the Republic, and again under the rule of Francisco Franco. In his personal file, he preserved the invitation of the academy, evidently as a curiosity. At the bottom of the page he had written "Ha, ha!" Later in life he stated his views on the academy more explicit. He said that membership in the institution could be considered in different ways—as a reward for merit, as material gain that would come from the increased sale of the member's books and as the guarantee of a comfortable chair with a number and a place to work. The company of academicians had increased so much in recent years, he said, that he had come to regard the academy as a casino for the aged and aging. "I have never been a member of any casino", he concluded.[9]

During his years in Moguer Jiménez saw personal and economic changes in the family, which was never to recover the solidarity and security it had enjoyed while the poet's father was living. His sisters married and established homes of their own. His mother moved from the house on Calle Nueva to a smaller one on another street of Moguer. The prosperity of the family declined as one after another of the vineyards and wineries were lost in costly litigation.[10]

IV   *La Soledad Sonora* (The Sonorous Solitude)

Between 1908 and 1912 Jiménez wrote and published four books of poetry, *La soledad sonora* (*The Sonorous Solitude*), 1911, *Poemas mágicos y dolientes* (*Magic and Sorrowful Poems*), 1911, *Melancolía* (*Melancholy*), 1912 and *Labertino* (*Labyrinth*), 1913.[11] It was the period of most complete isolation—"literary solitude", he called it—of his entire career as an author. Although he maintained correspondence with writers in Madrid, he lacked the stimulation of their company and conversation. In 1908, after several years in Paris, Darío returned to Madrid to serve as minister of Nicaragua at the Spanish court. However, he remained in Madrid only a little more than a year, and there was no meeting of the two poets during that time. The exchange of letters between them was much less regular than it had been before Jiménez' return to Moguer, although there was never a break in the friendship. *Melancholy* is dedicated to Rubén Darío, proof of Jiménez' continued admiration for the older poet.

The four books mentioned above mark no radical departure in style and content from those which immediately precede them, but there are in them signs of change. The melancholy of the earlier works persists, but it becomes increasingly an expression of spiritual tedium more than an outpouring of amorous or elegiac sentiment. Jiménez has often been called a Symbolist, and the designation is perhaps the most acceptable of any applied to his work in general. It is significant that the collection *Magic and Sorrowful Poems* is dedicated to Albert Samain, whose simple, tender lyrics quite understandably appealed to Jiménez. However, during the later years at Moguer, Baudelaire competes with Samain for a place in the poet's intimacy. The desperate sincerity and the corrosive pessimism of the French poet left their marks on many of the poems of the period.

The use of alexandrines becomes more frequent during the period, and in *Melancholy* this form is used exclusively. Commonly the poems have four line stanzas with assonance in the even lines, but *Melancholy* also introduces the alexandrine tercet, with uniform assonance in the three verses and often throughout the entire poem. Jiménez had by this time attained greater facility in the use of the fourteen syllable line, but there are still some lapses into the verbosity and imprecision to which the form seemed to lend itself.[12] The formal experiments of the period are few, and aside from such minor innovations as these tercets, they are of little importance.

The Sonorous Solitude is the most representative of the four collections of poems both in its faithfulness to Jiménez' innate vision of the world and in its presage of his maturity.[13] An epigraph by San Juan de la Cruz gives the book its title, and suggests the existence of a bond between the mystic poet and Jiménez. The title itself is an example of a stylistic feature, and perhaps also a psychological quirk, common to both poets, fondness for antithesis and paradox.[14] However, it is not until a later stage in Jiménez' poetic evolution that the real kinship between the two poets becomes clearly discernible. The solitude in *The Sonorous Solitude* is not that of withdrawal from the world but of intimate communion with the world; outer vision rather than inner. The adjective *sonora* (sonorous) in the title is appropriate, for there is perhaps more auditory imagery in these poems than in those of any other of Jiménez' works. The visual imagery runs the gamut of colors that in general characterize Jiménez' poetry of this period. Solitude permits the poet to discover the subtle enchantment in the natural world around him. Exceptional moments in the daily reality of his sensory experience are the source of the best poems in the volume. Recreated through his sensibility, this reality is endowed with new grace and splendor. However, the tranquility of this vision is often troubled by the old anxiety which intrudes again. One poem ends with this interrogation: "... what sun sheds on the garden grass this gleam / of death, which fades my eyes and my soul?" ("... qué sol pone en la hierba del jardín este brillo / de muerte, que destiñe mis ojos y mi alma?") [15]

This psychic duality appears in many of the poems of *The Sonorous Solitude*. The following verses, excerpted from one of the poems, offer a good example:

> Sky, bird, sun! While I live I want no more
> than this blue afternoon of harmony and gold!
>
> Oh that I could prolong eternally
> this instant of music, fragrance, and song.
>
> ¡Cielo, pájaro, sol! ¡No quiero, mientras viva,
> más que esta tarde azul, de armonía y de oro!
>
> ¡Ah, quien pudiera prolongar eternamente
> este instante de música, de fragrancia y de canto!

(PLP, 914)

The first two verses express the unfeigned delight of one awakened to full awareness of the beauty around him and to the realization that the present moment is sublime. "Sky, bird, sun!" is a cry of ecstasy, not a theme for elaboration. Adjectives would only encumber it. However, what follows is a different note, one that becomes insistent in a later period, the yearning to perpetuate the perfect instant and make it eternal. The last two verses anticipate the preoccupation with time which is so obsessive in the middle and declining years of the poet, the central theme of his so-called "second period", identified by Sánchez Barbudo as "el ansia de eternidad", the yearning for eternity. [16]

In *The Sonorous Solitude* there is a poem to a pine tree—unmistakably the one that stands by the house at Fuentepiña—in which the poet's contemplation of the "rhythmic verdure" attains a mystic rapture:

> ... My heart entranced,
> like the heart of a child laughs and weeps,
> enraptured in the infinite and limitless.

... Mi corazón suspenso,
igual que el corazón de un niño ríe y llora,
embelesado en lo infinito y en lo inmenso.

(PLP, 928)

The point of departure in the creation of the poem was clearly reality. The pine is a tree of a common species which the poet sees every day. However, its reality may vary from day to day, or hour to hour with morning or evening light, sun or shadow, wind or calm. It enters the poet's consciousness not only through his vision but also through his perception of its fragrance, the sound of its boughs in movement, the song of birds in its crown. The moment he apprehends in the poem is one in which the pine tree is resplendent in the sun, its branches reach into the depths of a blue sky, a breeze gives it a rhythmic movement and ripples of joyous song come from the birds in the dark green crown. The reality of the tree persists, but it is at once a marvel which nature may never again display in exactly the same way. The poet's reaction to it transcends his sensory awareness of the pine tree; he is transfigured, in tune with the infinite.

The poem might well have ended on this note, but Jiménez added a stanza expressing his wish that a pine tree grow by his tomb to shade and comfort him in death. Obviously the thought had come from Musset, whose poem "Lucie" Jiménez must certainly have known.[17] However, the closing stanza, whether borrowed or original, is an unnecessary postscript; its conventional Romanticism adds nothing to the poem.

A group of twenty-nine poems in *The Sonorous Solitude* under the title *"La flauta y el arroyo"* ("The Flute and the River") recaptures briefly some of the exuberance of *Ballads of Spring* and forms a pleasing interlude of affirmation in a period when disenchantment and tedium tend to dominate the poet's spirit. He abandons the artifice of the alexandrine to return to the more spontaneous *romance*. Many of the poems have the freshness of the streams and fountains which are the source of much of their imagery. Spanish poets, perhaps more than most others, have been fascinated by the sound, the movement, the reflection and the life-sustaining properties of water. This may be because most of Spain

is dry and sunny and water is precious. Jiménez attributed some of
his traits to Moorish ancestry, and the delight he experienced when
he saw the gleam of water through green foliage, heard it ripple
over stones or marveled at its transparency may have been one of
these atavistic influences. Anyone who has visited the gardens of
the Generalife and has heard the splashing of fountains, the
murmur of water in underground channels or its whisper as it races
through stone conduits cannot doubt that the Moors had an
unusual sensitivity to its sound and mystery.

The opening stanza of one of the poems of ''The Flute and the
River'' exemplifies the simplicity, the spontaneity and the pleasing
imagery of the collection:

> The water's song is silver,
> gold the poplar's rustle...,
> the music of my flute
> is of silver and of gold.

> La copla del agua es plata,
> oro la charla del chopo...,
> la música de mi flauta
> es de plata y es de oro.

                                                    (PLP, 965)

The ingenuous spirit of the ''The Flute and the River'' is that of a
child who delights in the unclouded present in a world of light,
fragrance and song. One poem evokes idyllic hours when nature,
love and God were in perfect harmony. It is a return to Eden:

> We were God, she and I,
> all things belonged to the three;
> the fountain, the white cloud,
> the grass, the butterfly.

> Eramos Dios ella y yo,
> de los tres fueron las cosas;
> la fuente, la nube blance
> la hierba, la mariposa.

                                                    (PLP, 963)

This serene joy is, of course, not a sustained note in the poetry of this period. Jiménez soon returns to the melancholy and tedium which he had momentarily forgotten. As if the alexandrine were the proper accompaniment to this mood, he resumes its use.

V   *Further Collections*

The collection *Poemas mágicos y dolientes* (*Magic and Sorrowful Poems*) begins with "Autumn", a poem, which is more artifice than art. The metaphors are particularly inept. Autumn is a "sad prince with "sky-blue eyes" and "golden hair", dressed in "black brocade". Fortunately such contrived imagery does not appear often, but there is, throughout this and the succeeding volumes of the same period, a stylistic affectation which diminishes their spontaneity and their depth, and which sometimes borders on the grotesque. In the final poem of *Labyrinth,* to cite an example, the scent of jasmine and the tender glances of the poet's love unite in one sensation, and he inquires whether it is her eyes that are fragrant with jasmine and sunlight.

Synesthesia, the literary interchange of the senses, was common in the Modernist period, and Jiménez makes abundant use of it during the Moguer years. The following examples, selected at random, are typical: "harmony of fragrant colors", "melody of light", smell of moonlight", "melodious flowers", "pensive mauve", "subdued and mauve sob". Although the sensory content of his poetry was sometimes enriched in this way, just as often Jiménez' infatuation with synesthesia resulted in his abuse of it. However, it may have been more meaningful to the poet himself than to most of his readers. His sensory perception was extremely keen, and he was disturbed or excited by sounds and smells that would have had little effect on most individuals. Much later in life he claimed that he could detect smells by telephone. No doubt there was more fantasy than fact in his assertions of this sort.

Critics have often referred to the impressionism of Jiménez' "first period", which embraces all his poetry written before 1916. If sensory content and imagery varied frequently with the interplay of colors and light are the identifying features, then the Moguer years mark the apogee of Jiménez' impressionism. It is significant

that after he had completed his secondary studies he seriously
considered making a career of painting. Colors delighted him, quite
independently of whatever symbolic values they might have. A
favorite toy of his childhood was the kaleidoscope, and as an
elderly man he was still fascinated by its limitless combinations of
colors and shapes.

In Moguer the fields, hills, trees, streams, flowers seen at different hours of the day offered as varied a spectacle as the
miniature one of the kaleidoscope. The poems written there are of
kaleidoscopic richness in their chromatic variety and range. Dawn
and late afternoon—when light, shadow and colors show their
greatest variations—were his favorite times of day. The following
brief poem, inspired by a Moguer dawn, is quite typical of Jiménez'
"impressionistic" manner.

> Lap of dawn! The mist is scarlet
> and the gossamer moon disappears in the blue...;
> the sea emerges new from the shadows, rose, silvery,
> the morning birds come to the green pine.
>
> And to the errant caress of the golden splendor
> that the new day casts on the pearly garden,
> beside the blue, clear fountain, I lament
> with the sweet unprinted rhyme of some dead poet.
>
> ¡Regazo de la aurora! La bruma es escarlata
> y la luna de gasa en el azul se pierde...;
> surge el mar de las sombras, nuevo, rosa, de plata,
> los matinales pajaros vienen al pino verde.
>
> y a la caricia errante del resplandor de oro
> que el nuevo día pone sobre el perlado huerto,
> al lado de la fuente celeste y clara, lloro
> la dulce rima inédita de algún poeta muerto...

> (PLP, 923)

The sensations of the first stanza are almost entirely visual and
chromatic and they are partially so in the second. However, what
might have been simply an impressionistic sketch becomes an elegy
when the poet's emotion intrudes, as it does in the last two verses.

Jiménez' predilection for certain colors is apparent particularly during the Moguer period. Gold (*oro*) is the one he obviously prefers to all others. Its frequent use in his poetry—not limited to any period but characteristic of all his work—has been the subject of many commentaries by critics.[18] Sometimes it occurs several times in a short poem. The following examples are taken from a twelve line poem in *Labyrinth* (PLP, 1282): "sad gold", "gold of peace and music", "gold of the melodious and grieving heart", "gold of eternity and poetry", "Illusion with wings of gold". Clearly *oro* is not simply descriptive of what is visible but has subjective connotations that go far beyond what is seen by the eyes. It *may* be used descriptively, but more commonly it gives an ideal dimension to the real, or it elevates to the highest degree of perfection, plenitude and beauty whatever it modifies. Throughout the history of mankind, gold has been prized for its unique physical properties as well as for the material value it came to have. It represented at once what was most beautiful and most valuable in the world. Jiménez retains its use as symbolic of beauty but transforms its objective values into purely abstract ones.

Rose, yellow, silver, blue, green and all the shades of purple—mauve, violet, amethyst, lilac—were prominent in Jiménez' impressionistic palette. He had his own "mauve decade", which embraced the years at Moguer, the period of his most markedly Decadent tendencies. The use of mauve (*malva*) is actually symptomatic of those tendencies. The word disappears from his vocabulary when the poet emerges from his morbid self-absorption and takes a new look at the world.

The collection *Melancholy* has a group of poems under the appropriate title of "Tenebrae". Although lugubrious sensuality and despondency, strongly reminiscent of Baudelaire, appear in all of Jiménez' books of this period, in these fifteen poems they are the dominant tone. The adjectives are consistently somber: black, broken, grim, sinister, empty, gloomy, dirty, false, cold, funereal, livid, leafless, leaden, etc. It is as if nature itself had fallen under a curse or were being consumed by some sinister blight. There is an occasional passage, such as the following, which anticipates surrealism:

> Passion has opened it all. Tragic forms
> flee, toward the west, in a sinister wind,
> and over the dry sand to a sea of blood go
> great lilies fallen from broken black vases...

Todo lo ha abierto la pasión...Trágicas formas
huyen, hacia el poniente, en un viento funesto,
y por la arena seca se van a un mar de sangre
grandes lirios caídos de rotos vasos negros...

(PLP, 1453)

Jiménez commonly dedicated his books, and groups of poems
within the books, to Spanish or Spanish-American contemporaries.
A complete list would include the names of many of the prominent
Hispanic writers of the time. The dedications to women—some
identifiable, others not—are also numerous especially in the books
written at Moguer. One in particular deserves mention, Francina,
said to have been a servant girl in the house of Dr. Lalanne, the
physician who attended Jiménez during his illness and con-
valescence in Bordeaux in 1901.[19] In *Pastorals* (1905) this dedication
appears: "To Francina, white flesh, lovely eyes, fine curls". In
Magic and Sorrowful Poems Francina reappears in a group of
seven poems in which the poet celebrates her beauty and ingenuous
charm with candid, sensual delight. She is another Eve before the
Fall. Although in later years Jiménez disowned most of the poetry
of his youth and early manhood, one of the poems to Francina has
been retained, with minor changes, in each of the anthologies he
published during his lifetime. It begins thus:

With lilacs drenched with water
I struck her over the back.

And all her white flesh
Was jeweled with shiny drops.

Con lilas llenas de agua,
le golpée las espaldas.

Y toda su carne blanca
se enjoyó de gotas claras.

(PLP, 1112)

During the years at Moguer Jiménez experienced both the
exhilaration and the torment of love. He was extremely susceptible

to both its sensual and its ideal appeal, but his passion was usually followed by disenchantment and often by bitterness and remorse. The theme is a common one in the poems of this period. In one he laments that he has found "hussies...instead of divine women!" ("Mujerzuelas...en vez de mujeres divinas!"). In another he apostrophizes: "Woman, carnal garden of sorry labyrinths, / you who bloody the sun of happy afternoons." ("Mujer, jardín carnal de tristes laberintos / que ensangrientas el sol de las tardes felices") (PLP, 1434).

Obviously, the joys of the salubrious rural life were by this time beginning to decline. Jiménez delighted in nature, but his enjoyment was more contemplative than active. He was not a Thoreau or a Frost. Despite his love of solitude, he was far from being independent of other human beings. The possibilities of finding kindred spirits, either in feminine or masculine society, were naturally limited in a provincial hamlet like Moguer. Both love and intellectual stimulation had given all they had to offer by the time he had been in Moguer three or four years. Intermittently he had also been in ill health. These circumstances explain the atmosphere of tedium, disillusionment and gloom that pervades much of his work between 1906 and 1912.

Poetry was a means of escaping from his depression, not the vital creative force it would become later. The innate sincerity and refinement of the poet were often defeated by a fatuous egocentricity which had possessed him during these years. His pampered childhood and youth, his early rise to fame and his cloistered existence were probably responsible for it. He wrote without interruption, but the quality of his poetry was uneven. Jiménez himself was dissatisfied and he longed for the day when his work would be perfected. Hatred, evil, affliction and death might prevail at last, but he would live in his finished work, his "book of gold".[20]

CHAPTER 4

Madrid: New Activity and Prestige

FROM 1912 until 1936 Jiménez lived in Madrid, returning only occasionally to Moguer for brief visits with his mother and other members of the family. His sister was now married and the old home had passed into other hands, the houses, vineyards and wineries the family once owned having been lost in litigation and foreclosures, largely the result of action taken by the Bank of Spain.[1] Friends in Madrid had urged the poet to return to the capital,[2] which he did, probably without any foreknowledge that he was never again to make his permanent home in Moguer.

I In the Residencia

For four years Jiménez lived at the Residencia de Estudiantes, the very center of the intellectual and literary life of Madrid, an institution recently created, but one of great activity and influence. The Residencia soon outgrew its original quarters on Fortuny Street and moved to a new location farther from the center of Madrid, a hill with a pleasant outlook known as "Cerro del Aire". The Residencia provided rooms for students and also for some of the writers, lecturers and teachers who participated in its activities. It had a good library and lecture rooms; it sponsored lectures, concerts, visits to art galleries, and published scholarly and creative works. The Residencia was frequented by Spain's best-known authors, artists and philosophers, and also attracted foreign writers and intellectuals. There Jiménez had occasion to see often such eminent Spaniards as Unamuno and Menéndez Pidal—both considerably older than he—as well as Antonio Machado, Ortega y Gasset and many others of his own generation. Among the students

62

were several who later attained fame in literature and art, notably García Lorca, Rafael Alberti and Salvador Dalí.[3]

During this period, one of transition in his literary evolution, Jiménez wrote two books of verse, *Sonetos espirituales* (*Spiritual Sonnets*) and *Estío* (*Summer*) and finished his prose masterpiece, *Platero y yo,* which he had begun in Moguer.[4] In form *Spiritual Sonnets* is unique among Jiménez' poetic works, for it alone employs the sonnet exclusively. He had matured considerably since his period of greatest formal experimentation. Dissatisfied with what he had produced during those years, he may have wished to atone for some of the excesses of the past, and also to convince himself that he could use a classic form with precision. A number of sonnets appear in his first two books, *Violet Souls* and *Water Lilies,* but like those of Darío, who in *Blue* had begun to vary the versification of the sonnet, the poems do not respect the classic pattern. There are alexandrine sonnets, the kind the Modernists in general found peculiarly appealing, as well as some with twelve, thirteen and sixteen syllable verses. However, in *Spiritual Sonnets* the eleven syllable verse is used uniformly [5] and the traditional rhyme scheme is also preserved. These poems are characterized by a high degree of technical perfection.

The restraint of form also imposed a greater emotional restraint in *Spiritual Sonnets* than in earlier volumes. These were the most intellectual poems that Jiménez had written up to this time. There is no essential change in themes or in imagery but there is now a greater serenity, a more decorous balance between thought and sentiment than before. The form, and the tradition that lay behind it, may have exposed Jiménez to another danger, the one that his compatriots of the seventeenth century found irresistible: verbal agility for its own sake. The love theme is particularly susceptible to treatment in this manner and can easily become a juggling of conceits rather than an expression of tenderness or passion.[6] Jiménez did not entirely elude this hazard. Yet what is apparent in the collection as a whole is a complete mastery of form, a great resourcefulness in maintaining both structural and verbal precision and refinement. The best of these sonnets are like finely cut gems, but because they are illuminated by a glow of emotion their brilliance is not the cold glitter that results from exclusive concern with intellectual subtlety and formal perfection.

The introductory poem, "To the Sonnet with my soul" ("Al

soneto con mi alma"), contains the essence of the volume—a statement of the intention, the esthetic orientation and the aspiration of the poet. The images appear in pairs, one the object, the other its abstraction: "wing"—"infinite flight"; "flower"—"errant essence"; "flame"—"splendor in movement"; "stream" [jet]—"coolness"; "diamond"—"noble richness"; etc. The physical image in each case is translated into a related ideal image, body and spirit, as is evident in the pair which occurs in the verse "thus in my *flesh* is the *total yearning*".[7] The succession of paired images culminates with those of the fountain and the reflected sky in its basin, figures which with aptness and beauty represent, respectively, the sonnet and the exalted sentiment it expresses. The pool of the fountain is limited by its perimeter of stone but it reflects the limitless sky. In like manner the sonnet, within the brevity and rigor of its form, reflects the infinite idealism of the poet's spirit.

The *Spiritual Sonnets* received considerable critical acclaim, but Jiménez abandoned the sonnet completely after this demonstration of virtuosity. There is no mystery about the choice, for the poet himself stated later, on a number of occasions, that he rejected the sonnet and fixed meter in general because the form tended to fetter the expression. Although he occasionally used regular meter, particularly the *romance*, from this point on there is no question about his preference for free verse.

The title of Jiménez' next volume of verse, *Estío* (*Summer*), may have been chosen for its connotation of maturity, ending a period of uncertainty and preparation, a view some critics have expressed.[8] At the time of its publication he was thirty-four, an age propitious for some sober reappraisal both of his work and of his attitudes. Even a casual reading of the volume suggests that a transition is taking place. These poems are brief and the verses which compose them are noticeably shorter than those of earlier compositions. The form is more varied and flexible. Rhyme occurs occasionally but not consistently. These externals are symptomatic of profounder changes. The adjective is now used with parsimony, not to adorn but to identify. Undoubtedly, Jiménez learned something about verbal economy from his experience writing *Spiritual Sonnets,* but in *Summer* his concern is not so much with stylistic renovation as with emotional truth. It is evident that *Summer* is a cathartic point both in his personal and his poetic evolution, although his total work retains a fundamental unity, unbroken at this stage or any subsequent one.

It would be impossible to explain what occurs in *Summer* without reference to the person whose influence was the most profound, sustained and beneficent of any that affected Jiménez and his work, and who, in effect, was largely responsible for the personal and esthetic transformation which began with *Summer.*

II   *Love and Engagement*

Jiménez met Zenobia Camprubí Aymar in Madrid in 1912. Not long afterward their engagement was formalized, although it was never officially announced, and few of the poet's acquaintances knew anything about it. Jiménez had been enamored of many women before, but invariably the experience had been followed by disillusionment, boredom or revulsion. Physical beauty appealed to him esthetically and sensually, but he could not long have endured anyone whose social assets were limited to a pretty face or figure, an empty head and frivolous conversation. Commonplaceness, insensitivity and vulgarity were all repellent to him.

Zenobia Camprubí was fair, blue-eyed and lovely, but she was also intelligent, spirited, sensitive and highly idealistic. She shared Jiménez' enthusiasm for literature, music and art. Her gaiety and inexhaustible kindness were an unfailing antidote for his morbidity. Zenobia's paternal grandfather was American and she had received some of her education in the United States, a circumstance which may explain another trait which her enamored fiancé found both engaging and frustrating, her independence of thought and conduct. She was probably less disposed than most Spanish women to submit to masculine caprice or domination.

In *Summer* love is an exalted sentiment which bears little resemblance to the petulant eroticism of such works as *Labyrinth* and *Melancholy.* The first brief poem of *Summer* is worth quoting, not so much for its merit—which is not exceptional—as for the new light in which it presents love:

You

All go by, green, scarlet...
You are there above, white.

All, noisy, fretful...
You are there above, serene.

All go by crafty, fickle...
You are there above, chaste.

Tú

Pasan todas, verdes, granas...
Tú estás allá arriba, blanca.

Todas, bullangueras, agrias...
Tú estás allá arriba, plácida.

Pasan, arteras, livianas...
Tú estás allá arriba, casta.

(LP, 81)

Adjectives and images of whiteness and purity are used frequently. Water, always an important source of imagery in Jiménez, is used with these connotations: "pure water of your chastity", "the fresh pure waters of your love". The spiritualization of love is reflected further in the reduction of the chromatic range of the images and the accentuation of their whiteness or transparency. Light becomes more important than color. In at least one poem it is identified with the one whom the poet loves: "when the day breaks / you are the light" ("Cuando rompe el día / la luz eres tú . . ."), strongly reminiscent of Bécquer ("poesía eres tú"). It is significant that in *Summer* the sun is the source of many images and the moon of very few. Light has suffused the poet's world, dispelled the shadows and consumed the mauve, the rose and opalescent mist that once enchanted him.

The same aspiration is evident in the impulse to be free of the ballast of sentimentality and sensuality that had up to this point kept the poet earthbound. He would have his written word effulgent "in the sun of the infinite day" like a "pure sword". The shining blade, like light in its beauty and brilliance, has, as well, its piercing and cleansing virtue. One is reminded of the common Spanish expression "Cortar por lo sano" ("to cut through the healthy [flesh]", i.e., to apply a drastic remedy), which implies a cutting to the quick, an elimination of what is decayed, tumescent and impure. In the same sense arrow (*flecha*), another piercing instrument, becomes an effective metaphor in *Summer* but with the added connotation of ascent, loftiness of aspiration.

Despite his idealization of love in *Summer,* Jiménez did not elevate it to a plane of abstraction remote from human experience. *Summer* expresses the excitement, the impatience, the loneliness, the despair and the tenderness of love. The view of love in these poems is markedly different from that in such works as *Labyrinth* or *Melancholy.* In one short poem love is, metaphorically, both a flower and new-born child which the poet holds in his arms by day, and over which he keeps affectionate and solicitous vigil by night. The first stanza of the poem follows:

> All the day, love, I hold
> your heart in my arms
> —oh white, infinite flower!—
> rocking it, caressing it.

> Todo el día tengo, amor,
> tú corazón en mis brazos
> —¡oh blanca flor infinita!—
> meciéndolo, acariciándolo.

(LP, 107)

Perhaps no other work of Jiménez' surpasses *Summer* as an exaltation and an affirmation of love.

III *Marriage*

On January 3, 1916 Jiménez sailed from Cádiz for New York, where Zenobia Camprubí had agreed to meet him, and where they were married on March 6. The poet and his bride remained in the United States until early June—his first visit—then returned to

Spain. Before the year ended Jiménez had published what he called *Diario de un poeta recién casado* (*The Diary of a Newly Married Poet*),[9] a book of compositions in free verse with brief prose poems interspersed, inspired by his sea voyages and his marriage.

The *Diary* is generally recognized as one of Jiménez' key works, a summit in his poetic evolution. Critics quite often speak of his "first period", their rather arbitrary designation for everything Jiménez wrote before the *Diary*; and of his "second period", a new manner initiated by that work. The poet's own estimate of the *Diary* is—somewhat surprisingly—in agreement with that of the critics. He called it "my best work", an opinion he still held thirty years after its publication.[10]

The *Diary* is made up of six groups of poems, each with an identifying title: "Hacia el mar" ("Toward the Sea"), "El amor en el Mar" ("Love on the Sea"), "America del este" ("Eastern America"), "Mar de retorno" ("Sea of Return"), "España" ("Spain"), "Recuerdos de America del este" ("Memories of Eastern America Written in Spain"). These titles are a little misleading, for the *Diary* is not simply a lover's diary nor a book of travel impressions. The work has a metaphysical dimension which sets it apart from preceding volumes, in which there is only occasionally a hint of this. Although the *Diary* contains a number of love poems, love is actually a secondary theme. Two of Jiménez' recent experiences affected him profoundly and were mainly responsible for the new trends in his poetry. One of these was the ocean voyage to New York and back to Spain again; the other was Jiménez' first direct contact with the United States.

Responsive as Jiménez was to all of the phenomena of nature, it was inevitable that his first travel by sea should affect him profoundly and suggest new possibilities of poetic expression. In childhood and youth he had lived near the sea, but traveling over it for several successive days and nights was something quite different from viewing it from the shore, just as flying would be vastly more exhilarating than simply looking at the sky from some point on the ground. It has been said that the sea imagery and symbolism in Jiménez derives from Valéry, an inaccurate judgment based, apparently, on Jiménez' fondness for Valéry's "Le cimetiére marin". Aside from the chronological discrepancy—the *Diary* was published in 1917 and "Le cimetiére marin" in 1920—there is no reason to credit Valéry with what was essentially a very personal reaction on the part of Jiménez to a new and stimulating experience.[11]

The vastness and the loneliness of the sea were sensations which at first possessed the poet. He was overwhelmed by the monotony of an endless expanse of gray water merging with a gray sky. However, it was the restless movement of the sea that fascinated him most. The unceasing motion—like the throbbing of an enormous cosmic heart—endued the sea with life, but unlike all the life that he had previously known, the sea escaped the curse of temporality. Its cold heart would beat forever. A brief poem simply and appropriately entitled "Mar" ("Sea") is addressed directly to the sea, as to a living force or being, the only one the poet had ever known over which time appeared to have no dominion:

> But a moment!
>
> Yes, sea, could I but be
> Like you, each instant changing,
> Oblivion spanned by heaven;
> Mighty sea—without decline!—
> Serene sea—
> With cold heart and eternal soul—
> Sea, persistent image of the present!
>
> ¡Sólo un punto!
>
> Sí, mar, ¡quien fuera,
> cual tú, diverso cada instante,
> coronado de cielos en su olvido;
> mar fuerte—¡sin caídas!—
> mar sereno
> —de frío corazón con alma eterna—,
> ¡mar, obstinada imagen del presente!

(LP, 258)

It is doubtful that any previous experience of the poet had led him to such significant discoveries. The power and the serenity of the sea were, of course, nothing new to him nor, for that matter, to the rest of humanity, but he had probably never seen the sea before as a part of the physical world which changed perpetually yet remained essentially unchanged, eternal. He must also have been elated over the discovery of the superlative paradox, the sea as a symbol both of mutability and constancy.

In the second group of "sea poems", those entitled "Sea of Return", there is an intensification of the emotional and creative excitement perceptible in the first group. Such poems as "Mar despierto" ("Wakeful Sea"), and "Partida" ("Departure") are evidence that Jiménez was scarcely exaggerating when he stated in his brief preface to the *Diary* that he composed these poems in the white heat of emotion ("frenético de emoción"). He wrote entranced by the revelation that the sea, a mighty throbbing heart, was immune to fatigue, decline and death, the sinister forces that made each man's life a burden of anguish to bear. Each day and night of his journey he—human and finite—was awed by the limitless panorama of sky, clouds, sun, moon, stars; but for the sea in which they were copied, the cosmic spectacle of beauty would be eternal. In none of his previous works had Jiménez captured with comparable fullness and intensity the vision of eternal beauty; in only one of his later works, *Animal de fondo* (*Animal of Depth*), 1949 was he again to attain this exalted and affirmative tone.

Before the trip to the United States, Jiménez had assimilated the conventional Spanish attitudes toward American civilization. These had been modified somewhat by his associations with Zenobia, but they had probably not prepared him for the real experience of the American environment. His impressions were recorded in the prose poems of the two divisions of the *Diary* entitled "Eastern America" and "Memories of Eastern America". The poet was both repelled and enchanted by what he saw in his wanderings through the streets of New York and on his excursions to points beyond the city, to Boston and Washington. He reacted with irony and humor to the sordidness, noise, offensive sights and smells, the bad taste, the oddity and absurdity of mores he observed around him, but he found much that appealed to him humanly and poetically. New York was both ugly and beautiful, always stimulating. In the compositions which it inspired there are implicit protests against grotesqueness, ugliness and dehumanization, but there are also a surprising number of passages notable for their beauty and their human appeal.[12]

The three and one half months in the United States brought Jiménez into an environment unlike any he had known before. Fortunately he did not withdraw from it—which seemed to be his natural impulse—but explored it with interest and absorption. The *Diary* reflects this new experience, the emergence from the isolation in which his earlier works were created. In the *Diary* there is a greater awareness of humanity, not in the abstract, but in the particular, and acceptance of the vulgar and the repugnant, as well as of the delicate and the sublime. The attitude is noticeable in the themes and the diction, both more varied and more vital than those of previous books. The several references in the *Diary* to American writers are indicative also of a broadening of Jiménez' literary acquaintance with America. As one would expect, the names include those of Poe, Whitman and Mark Twain, whom he had undoubtedly read before coming to the United States. What is more significant is the mention of such contemporaries as Robert Frost, Amy Lowell, Vachel Lindsay, Edgar Lee Masters and Edwin Arlington Robinson. His devotion to Emily Dickinson is evidenced by his inclusion in the *Diary* of three brief poems of hers in translation. Another American, Archer M. Huntington, founder and director of The Hispanic Society in America, sponsored the publication of Jiménez' first anthology. *Poesías escogidas* (Selected Poems), which appeared in 1917. One of the prose poems in the *Diary* is dedicated to Mr. Huntington.

In Jiménez' letters there is occasional mention of the World War of 1914-1918, but since Spain itself was neutral and rather far from the areas of combat, there was little disruption there of the normal manner of living. The years immediately following his marriage and return to Spain were perhaps the most peaceful and productive of any period in the poet's life. After a brief visit to Moguer, he and Zenobia set up their household in Madrid and soon were absorbed in new activities. Together they translated Rabindranath Tagore from the English, continuing a collaborative project which they had begun before their marriage. The poems and plays of the Indian author, with whom Jiménez felt a close kinship, became known in the Spanish-speaking world largely through these translations.

IV *Other Works of the Second Period*

Between 1918 and 1923 Jiménez published four important books of poetry: *Eternidades* (*Eternities*), *Piedra y cielo* (*Rock and Sky*), *Belleza* (*Beauty*), and *Poesía (en verso)* (*Poetry* [*in Verse*]). His *Segunda Antología Poética* (*Second Poetic Anthology,* 1898-1918) appeared during the same period. It enjoyed wide circulation, and several later editions of it were printed.

Eternities bears the simple dedication "To my wife", recognition which scarcely seems commensurate with Zenobia's talent, her remarkable versatility and exceptional merits. She was the poet's companion, nurse, secretary, translator, critic and interpreter—loyal, loving, cheerful, untiring—throughout their forty years of married life. However, Jiménez was fully cognizant of his dependence on Zenobia and of all that he owed to her. Behind the laconic dedication was no lack of generosity or gratitude but rather a rejection of effusiveness and sentimentality. One of the literary sins of his earlier years had been overstatement; he now atoned with understatement.

Two frequently quoted poems of *Eternities* are of particular interest as conscious expression of a new esthetic orientation. The first of these begins:

> Intelligence, give me
> the exact name of things!
> ...Let my word be
> the thing itself,
> created by my soul anew...

> ¡Inteligencia, dáme
> el nombre exacto de las cosas!
> ...Que mi palabra sea
> la cosa misma
> creada por mi alma nuevamente...

(LP, 553)

The poet here affirms a new recognition of the intellect in poetic creation, not necessarily subordinating emotion to it but considering one as the complement of the other in the composition of a poem. The emphasis on poetry as creation, not imitation or embellishment, was one of the principal tenets of Creationism—then ascendant—whose chief exponent, the Chilean poet Vicente Huidobro, enjoined his fellow poets not to sing of the rose but to make it bloom in the poem.[13]

The second composition, in which poetry itself is the theme, actually traces the evolution of Jiménez' own work, metaphorically identified as a woman. She first comes to him pure and "clothed in innocence", but soon she loses her ingenuous charm, arrays herself with ostentatious splendor and becomes a "gaudy queen". The love he once felt for her now changes to anger and aversion. Finally poetry divests herself of her splendid raiment and stands before the poet naked. This is the sublime moment of his life devoted to poetry: "Oh passion of my life, naked poetry, mine forever". The poetry-woman metaphor is sustained throughout the poem. Both in the vital and the esthetic sense woman represented to Jiménez the superlative in grace and beauty, as her presence in the poetry of this and following periods clearly testifies. However, she has emerged from the erotic miasma that once enveloped her. There is little sensuality in the adjective "naked" as Jiménez now uses it. It denotes rather authenticity, purity, grace, beauty, unveiled and without blemish. Thus Jiménez relives his own poetic experience. The early innocence is, ostensibly, an allusion to the period when Bécquer was his idol; the "gaudy queen" refers most plausibly to the external brilliance and sense appeal of the Modernists and the Decadents; the "nakedness" of the third period is simply the essentiality of pure poetry.

To Jiménez pure poetry was not what some of his contemporaries, descendants of Mallarmé, understood it to be. He did not consider emotion to be an impurity but the very source of poetry. The intellect refined the expression but did not furnish the initial impulse of the poem. It is not surprising, then, that *Eternities* contains many love poems, comparable in their intensity to those of the *Diary* and *Summer*. Conjugal love, not a popular theme or a profound sentiment in poets generally, is the source of many of Jiménez' poems. *Eternities* is affirmative in tone to such an extent that one critic speaks of its "optimism" as one of its clearly distinguishing features.[14] The yearning for an elusive happiness now gone and the anguish over an unknown future are powerless to cloud the present, a time of plenitude and fulfillment. For once the beauty of reality is unsurpassed by that of dreams. Body and soul are in tune, like a "matchless thought" in a "perfect verse", as one poem puts it.

The use of the plural *Eternities* suggests that Jiménez saw more

than one possibility of transcending the temporal. However, the
preoccupation with time is less obsessive in this book than in his
other works generally. He looks at death with serenity, not as a
terrifying uncertainty, but as restful oblivion:

> Oblivion, solitude; so pleasing
> here, awake; oblivion, solitude eternal;
> how divine you must be to those asleep
> forever!

> ¡Olvido, soledad; tan gratos
> aquí, despierto; olvido, soledad, eternos;
> qué divinos seréis a los dormidos
> para siempre!

> (LP, 678)

In another poem Jiménez calls sleep "...sweet apprenticeship /
of the definitive oblivion" ("Sueño, dulce aprendizaje del
definitivo olvido"—(*Eternities,* p. 114). The works of this period
contain many such poems within poems, short, sententious
passages—usually metaphysical and imagistic—resembling haikus
in their concision and delicate imagery.[15] Comparing his mature
style with the earlier manner—*Eternities, Beauty, Rock and Sky*
with *Labyrinth* and *Melancholy*—it is apparent that Jiménez has
subjected his poetic idiom to a rigorous elimination both of
rhetorical and sentimental excesses. It gains in essentiality,
profundity and universality.

The relative stability of this period of Jiménez' life is attributable
to a combination of fortunate circumstances: a happy marriage,
good health—which he mentions sometimes in letters to his
mother—, literary success, prestige and intellectual stimulation. He
is too involved in life to brood over death. Concomitantly, there is
no intense expression of religious sentiment in *Eternities.* However,
the poet's aspiration to transcend the temporal and the terrestrial
through his word, the attainment of immortality in the poem, is
clearly voiced. The volume ends on this note:

> Eternal word of mine!
> Oh, what supreme living
> —my tongue and lips now in nothingness—,

oh, what supreme living
of flower· without stalk and without root,
sustained by light, and with my memory,
alone and fresh in the air of life!

Palabra mía eterna!
!Oh, qué vivir supremo
—ya en la nada la lengua de mi boca—
oh, qué vivir divino
de flor sin tallo y sin raíz,
nutrida, por la luz, con mi memoria,
sola y fresca en el aire de la vida!

(LP, 688)

Rock and Sky, Beauty and *Poetry* (*in Verse*) are related to
Eternities in theme, style, intellectual and emotional content. *Rock
and Sky* begins with three brief poems each entitled "The Poem",[16]
an indication that now, more consciously than ever before, Jiménez
is seeking the vehicle with which to express the ineffable—for he
defined poetry as "the expression of the ineffable"—a debilerate
contradiction in terms which stated rather effectively what he
hoped to achieve. The aspiration is evident in the opening verses of
one of these poems: "Song of mine, / Sing before singing..."
(Canción mía, canta, antes de cantar). The poem, then exists
ideally before it is written. It is the impulse, the emotion and grace
which the poet must transmit to his readers through the written
word, transcending somehow the written word. The mind does not
supply the spontaneous constituent but only channels it or refines
it. "Enthusiasm taken through the prism of the intellect", one of
Robert Frost's definitions of poetry, comes close to Jiménez'
esthetic posture during this period.

The poet's awareness of his destiny as a creator is readily
discernible in *Eternities,* but it becomes more accentuated in the
succeeding volumes. His Work (*Obra*), which he now spells with a
capital letter, is often his theme, particularly in *Beauty* and *Poetry*
(*In Verse*). His success, prestige without decline, and his influence,
now powerful throughout the Hispanic world, must have
strengthened his conviction that his work would be an imperishable
legacy, that he would live through it and that there was urgency in

perfecting it. *Beauty* begins with a poem in which Jiménez likens his Work to a "painting in the air", which time will obliterate, leaving only the silence and oblivion of un unknowing universe. However, an impulse more powerful than reason asserts that his Work will survive beyond the limitations of time, space and mortality, that it will attain a limitless existence, unattainable beauty ("imposible norma bella"). The poem closes with an apostrophe beginning "Mortal, immortal flower of mine..." a rather typical antithesis, synonymous here with the Work—and in a sense, a defiance of the rational exigencies of written language as well as of the disturbing realities of existence.

One of the most significant changes observable in Jiménez' second period is precisely the awareness of the transcendental power of his own poetry. "And death shall have no dominion", a verse from Dylan Thomas, might aptly be applied to the new consciousness that brought Jiménez a measure of relief from the uncertainty that had tormented him earlier. In a poem entitled "La Obra" ("The Work") (*Beauty,* p. 139), he speaks of death's separation of himself, the mortal man, from his "immortal son". Death will, in effect, be an opening of "the gates of larger life", the mortal body merely an abandoned shell, the annunciation of the zenithal fruition, of timeless plenitude. A poem in *Poetry (in Verse)*—quoted in part below—expressed the sustaining conviction in a series of contrasting yet complementary images:

> Beside my dead body
> my living work.
>
>   The day
> of my complete life
> in nothing and in all,
> —the closed flower with the open flower—
>
> ....
>
> ineffable maternal sleep
> of the discarded husk and dry cocoon,
> beside the eternal fruit,
> and the infinite butterfly!
>
> Al lado de mi cuerpo muerto,
> mi obra viva.

                    El día
de mi vida completa
en la nada y el todo,—la flor cerrada con la abierta flor—;

....

inefable dormirse maternal
de la cáscara vana y del capullo seco,
al lado del eterno fruto
y la infinita mariposa!

(LP, 963)

The recognition of the creative power of the intellect in the poetic process ("Intelligence give me / the exact name of things") marked a turning point in Jiménez' esthetic evolution, but without resulting in his rejection of what he had always held to be the very source of poetry. Emotion continued to be the impulse that produced his poems. Religious preoccupation, not often expressed in his works written between 1900 and 1916, was, nevertheless, always latent in his spirit during those years.[17] In the following period, rather than receding, it became a more insistent, although now a more reasoned inquiry into the meaning of existence. His early religious training in the home and in a Jesuit school undoubtedly conditioned his thinking throughout his life, leaving him a distaste for orthodox Catholicism,[18] but also with an insatiable longing for continuity in a sublimer state than this ephemeral existence. The awareness of this possibility must have come through the church. Jiménez could not accept nonexistence, total oblivion, as the end of man. The poem quoted above, and a number of others contemporary with it, suggest that his non-doctrinal Christianity may have been modified by contacts with Hinduism.[19] The "discarded husk" which becomes "eternal fruit" is reminiscent of the "Seed imperishable" of Hindu religious thought. When Jiménez speaks of his "complete life / in nothing and in all" his words seem an echo of others, attributed to Krishna: "...immortality and also death, being and non-being am I."[20] The parallel probably points to nothing more radical in Jiménez' religious thinking than a sort of poetic eclecticism that enabled him to select or reject in religion whatever pleased or displeased him temperamentally and esthetically, just as he did in everything else.

It is quite apparent in *Poetry* and in Jiménez' other works of the same period that his conception of an existence beyond the present life is not simply an aspiration for his work to survive and exert its influence after his physical death, the sort of circumscribed immortality of which Vigny spoke in "La bouteille à la mer". This, of course, like all authors, he desired, but this alone did not satisfy him. His passion was for imperishable beauty and for his own continuity at one with that beauty. The sentiment is expressed in poems like the following:

The Green Bird

Down the river I go,
wherever the water wishes,
between the two shores.

From the two shores,
how I watch myself going downstream,
at peace in all the beauty
I pass—what has been!

Good-by, good-by! How pleasing to go
when one remains in all.

El pajarito verde

En el río me voy,
adonde quiera el agua,
entre las dos orillas.

Desde las dos orillas
¡cómo me miro yo bajando por el agua,
quieto en todo lo bello
que paso—lo que fué...—

¡Adiós, adiós! ¡Que grato el irse,
cuando se queda uno en todo!

(LP, *Poetry,* 939)

The final poem of *Poetry* ends on a similar note, an affirmation of belief in an extratemporal consciousness, a sort of quiescent immortality, of oneness within a great totality ("uno en lo uno") embracing man and nature, being and nonbeing.

V *Success and Influence*

The succession of poetic works from the *Diary* (1916) to *Poetry* (*in Verse*) (1923) assured Jiménez of a position of pre-eminence in Spanish poetry of that period. Neither Unamuno nor Antonio Machado, great as was their prestige, overshadowed him. Had he been of less ardent and restless spirit he might have been satisfied with the measure of poetic immortality he had by this time attained. However, he continued his assiduous literary activity, although circumstances more than design determined the direction it was to take. He edited several short-lived literary magazines: *Indice* (1921-1922), *Sí* (1925) and *Ley* (1927). A list of the contributors would include many of the most distinguished Spanish writers of the day, and some of those of Spanish America. Conscious of the position of leadership to which he had involuntarily been elevated, he took notice of the younger writers and encouraged those who showed promise. His approval often meant an auspicious introduction to the literary world. In addition to the magazines he edited briefly, Jiménez published poems, essays and "lyric portraits" in "notebooks" (*cuadernos*), as he called them, beginning with *Unidad* (*Unity*) in 1925 and continuing with the series *Sucesión* (*Succession*) and *Presente* (*Present*) of 1932 and 1933 respectively.

There was virtually no poet of the talented generation of 1927 who was not in some way indebted to Jiménez. Federico García Lorca's initial success in Madrid, where he arrived relatively unknown in 1919, can be attributed in large measure to Jiménez' influence and support. In *Indice* Jiménez published poems by Lorca and also by Pedro Salinas and Jorge Guillén, who were still unknown to the Spanish public.[21] Jiménez warmly praised Rafael Alberti's book, *Marinero en tierra* (1925), thus practically assuring him of a position of prestige in contemporary Spanish poetry. The role of poetic arbiter that Rubén Darío had played earlier in the century had now fallen to Jiménez. Alberti's appraisal of Jiménez expresses quite accurately the opinion held generally by poets of his

generation: "In those enthusiastic years in Madrid Juan Ramón
Jiménez was to us, even more than Antonio Machado, the man
who had elevated poetry to a religion, living exclusively by and for
it, dazzling us with his example...." [22]

Somewhat like Unamuno, who earlier in the century had
ridiculed the Modernists and inveighed against the Francophilia of
his compatriots, Jiménez now found fault with those who were
dazzled and subverted by the innovations introduced by the
vanguard poets. He was sensitive to the esthetic changes of the day
but saw no merit in novelty for novelty's sake, least of all superficial imitations of foreign works. In his own poetry he achieved
originality, not in defiance of tradition, but consonant with it, a
harmonious synthesis of tradition and change. He was both a
restraining and a stimulating influence. The *Romancero,* the Arab-
Andalusian poets, the mystics and popular poetry constituted a
treasure of poetic resources which could scarcely be exhausted, and
no Spaniard of his time was more cognizant of the fact than
Jiménez. Ultraism, Creationism, Dadaism and Futurism attracted
some of Jiménez' contemporaries—Gerardo Diego, Antonio
Espina, Guillermo de Torre to mention a few of them—but there
was no radical break with the past. Apollinaire, Huidobro, Tzara,
Marinetti, Breton and their partisans were not a serious challenge
to the position of Jiménez, Antonio Machado and Unamuno.
Conversely, San Juan de la Cruz, Góngora and Bécquer were still
living forces in Spanish poetry. The "Generation of 1927" owed
its name to Góngora, whose third centenary was celebrated in 1927
and whose virtuosity was admired and emulated by many poets of
this period. Jiménez who, perhaps unwittingly, was partly
responsible for the neo-Gongorist trend soon reacted with some
annoyance to its persistence and to the insinuation that he himself
was a Gongorist. [23]

Jiménez was not prepared by temperament, age—he was forty-
four in 1925—or inclination to be a benevolent grandfatherly
oracle of esthetics or mediator of the literary questions of his times.
He was only eleven years older than Salinas, twelve years older than
Guillén. Lorca and Vincente Aleixandre were his juniors by
seventeen years, Alberti and Luis Cernuda by twenty-one. José
Moreno Villa and León Felipe were practically his contemporaries.
He declared in one of his aphorisms that he proposed to "en-
courage the young, to reprove the mature, to tolerate the old". In

practice he lambasted all three, for he could not resist the diabolical impulse to use his finely barbed irony on those with whom he lost patience. He was not too young or too old to be immune to their counterattacks. More than one friendship was soured by these exchanges. Jorge Guillén and Luis Cernuda, to cite two notable examples, won the early approval of Jiménez, but later he feuded with both of them, the dispute with Guillén becoming particularly acrimonious. Cernuda appears never to have forgotten nor forgiven the differences he had with Jiménez and, like Salvador Rueda in the controversy with Rubén Darío, he kept airing his grievances after the death of his adversary.[24] The friendship with Gómez de la Serna and with Rafael Alberti also cooled. Even the amiable Pedro Salinas felt the sting of Jiménez' needling criticism.

Madrid in the twenties and thirties was, and still is, not only the literary capital of Spain but also its chief center of literary gossip. The rumor mills were rarely idle. The personal affairs, the foibles and crotchets of a writer, often amplified or distorted, were common topics of conversation. Jiménez, who shunned conventional social gatherings and had little time for chitchat, did his best to escape from the curious and importunate. He and Zenobia moved several times during their years of residence in Madrid. According to Alberti, Jiménez often answered the telephone himself, and when someone called from the concierge's booth announcing a visit or requesting an interview the poet would reply that he was not at home.[25] Madrileños were both annoyed and intrigued by Jiménez. The quiet gravity of demeanor, the sensitive features, the depth and the glow of his eyes, the black beard reminded many of paintings by El Greco. The Mexican essayist and poet, Alfonso Reyes, who was his friend and saw him often in Madrid, was one of the first to comment on the resemblance. Reyes also compared him to Góngora.

He is a spiritual relative of Góngora. His features remind one of him. Sometimes he smiles, but there is something forbidding in his smile, as if he were about to bite. Juan Ramón is implacable and pure. He can't abide what isn't perfect. He turns his back on all men he doesn't fully esteem. When he shakes hands he seems to be giving a verdict of approval.... [26]

In his brief sketch Reyes delineated with incisive accuracy the Jiménez he knew in the twenties. The latter was a severe critic, not only of others but of himself. By judging his contemporaries with the same uncompromising standards that he applied to himself he antagonized many of them. Their resentment was compounded by his sardonic quips and by his withdrawal from their society.

In 1936 Jiménez began an ambitious project, the preparation of an edition of his complete works, classified and arranged by himself. Only the first volume, *Canción* (*Song*)—a gleaning from the short lyrics he had written from early manhood to maturity—was ever published. The outbreak of the civil war disrupted his work and forced him and Zenobia to seek refuge abroad. Spain's writers and intellectuals were scattered to the four winds. Many found their way to America. Others were less fortunate, among them García Lorca, Unamuno and Antonio Machado, none of whom survived the Spanish Civil War.

Canción (*Song*), a favorite of Zenobia's, is the most extensive collection of short lyric poems Jiménez ever published, excepting, of course, his anthologies. The volume contains some new poems but also a large number that had appeared in earlier collections such as *Summer, Rock and Sky, Poetry, Beauty.* Some were to reappear in later books, notably *Voces de mi copla* (*Voices of My Song*) and *Estación total* (*Total Season*). *Song* is as felicitous a selection of brief lyric poems as Jiménez ever put together in one volume. Luis Vivanco comments accurately that in the four hundred-odd pages of *Song* there is almost an uninterrupted succession of poems of delightful imagery and sentiment, a vision of the immediate reality of the poet's world of sun, moon, birds, water, woman expressed with freshness, joy and profundity. The effective use of assonance in the majority of these poems amplifies and diversifies their prosodic structure and enhances their musical quality.[27] Vivanco points out that in *Song* Jiménez retains what is most profound and universal in Andalusian poetic tradition, an opinion very much like that expressed by Rubén Darío, more than fifty years earlier when he discovered the universal values in *Sad Airs* and dubbed Jiménez "the universal Andalusian".

CHAPTER 5

The New World

WHEN Jiménez and his wife left Spain in the late summer of 1936 the civil war was in its early stages. They could hardly have foreseen how profoundly and tragically the war was to affect the entire nation, and the extent to which it was to change their own lives. The poet had declined a diplomatic post offered him by Manual Azaña, president of the Spanish Republic, but he agreed to go to Washington, D. C. as honorary cultural attaché to the Spanish Embassy there. However, the war and the precarious state of the republican government rendered this cultural mission ineffectual and meaningless. The Jiménez' remained in the United States less than a month. Since it was now impossible to return to Spain, the best course for them to follow seemed to be to go to Puerto Rico, where Zenobia had family connections and friends.

In Puerto Rico Jiménez began what was to be a long and very significant personal participation in the literary and cultural life of Spanish America. Although his first visit to Puerto Rico was brief, lasting scarcely two months, he lectured at the university in Río Piedras and in several other cities of the island. Long regarded by his countrymen as a sort of high priest of Spanish poetry—"dictator" according to some of them[1]—it soon became evident that his prestige and influence were equally great in the Spanish-speaking countries of the New World. Long ago his talent had been extolled by the most admired of all Spanish-American authors, Rubén Darío and José Enrique Rodo. Now Spanish Americans were to see and hear Jiménez for the first time. The remaining twenty-two years of his life would be spent in the New World. During these years more of his works were to be printed in Buenos Aires, Mexico and Havana than in Madrid and Barcelona. His poems, articles and letters appeared in all the leading journals and the literary supplements of Spanish-American newspapers:

Nosotros, Sur, La Nación (Argentina): *El hijo pródigo, Cuadernos americanos, Revista mexicana de literatura* (Mexico); *El repertorio americano* (Costa Rica); *La Torre, Asomante* (Puerto Rico); *Atenea, Letras* (Chile); *Revista de América, Revista de las Indias, El tiempo* (Columbia); *Revista cubana, Orígenes* (Cuba); *El nacional, Cultura universitaria* (Venezuela); *Marcha* (Uruguay), etc. The complete list would be far too extensive to include here. There was probably not a single Spanish-American periodical or newspaper of consequence—excluding, of course, purely professional journals—which did not publish poems, aphorisms, essays, letters by Jiménez, with or without his permission. He was understandably irked by those who did not bother to obtain his permission to reprint his poems and prose pieces. He sometimes grumbled about the irresponsibility of Latin Americans, as if he considered all of them to be generously endowed with this trait.

After leaving Puerto Rico the Jiménez visited Cuba, the poet having been invited by the Institución Hispanocubana de Cultura to give a series of lectures under its sponsorship. In the cordial atmosphere of the Caribbean country Jiménez—now virtually an exile from his own country—collaborated enthusiastically with the writers and intellectuals who surrounded him. At his suggestion an anthology of contemporary Cuban poetry was compiled from selections submitted in a nationwide poetry contest. Jiménez was one of the judges, and he also wrote the introductory essay for the volume, *La poesía cubana en 1936* (*Cuban Poetry in 1936*).[2] This collection was made up of poems by sixty-three Cuban writers, among them some who already had won acclaim, and others who were subsequently to achieve wide recognition in Cuba and other countries of Spanish America: Nicolás Guillén, Regino Pedroso, José Lezama Lima, Emilio Ballagas, Mariano Brull, Dulce María Loynaz, Eugenio Florit and others. All were indebted to Jiménez for his interest and encouragement, and perhaps most of all for his example. Affinity of temperament and esthetic ideals established a felicitous rapport between him and some of the poets considerably younger than he. This was true of Ballagas and Florit in particular, and to some extent of Brull, excluding, of course, his Dadaist penchant.

What was happening in Cuba and Puerto Rico was taking place in all Spanish America. Perhaps no Spanish-speaking poet since Rubén Darío exerted a wider influence than Jiménez in Spanish

America.[3] The only other Spanish-speaking countries he was ever to visit were Argentina and Uruguay, in 1948. Efforts to entice him to Mexico, Peru, Chile, Colombia, Brazil and other Latin-American countries were unsuccessful. After his return from Buenos Aires and Montevideo, where he had been feted, applauded and honored as never before, Jiménez considered making a similar poetic tour of the cities on the Pacific side of the continent. However, when obstacles—real or imaginary—presented themselves he soon abandoned the project, but without in any way diminishing his prestige in America.

About the same time that Cuban poets were experiencing a surge of enthusiasm and creativity, stimulated by the presence of Juan Ramón Jiménez among them, talented young poets in Colombia, also under his banner, were renovating Colombian poetry. They were known as the "Piedraicielistas", a word coined from the title of one of Jiménez' books of poems, *Piedra y cielo* (Rock and Sky).[4] Those among them most closely identified with Jiménez esthetically were Eduardo Carranza and Jorge Rojas. Arturo Camacho Ramírez, another member of the group, was attracted more toward Surrealism and Pablo Neruda. Others diverged in various ways, but it is significant that they chose one of Jiménez' books as a model and an identifying symbol for all.[5]

The "Contemporaries" of Mexico are perhaps the most distinguished generation of poets that Spanish America has produced in the twentieth century.[6] All were young men, most of them not yet twenty, when the turbulent decade of the Mexican Revolution ended in 1920. They published their first works when the vanguard furor was gaining momentum throughout Latin America. However, they wisely refrained from mixing politics and poetry, and they were not carried away by enthusiasm for the more extreme forms of vanguardism. One of the "Contemporaries", Jaime Torres Bodet, comments on the indebtedness of this group to Antonio Machado and Juan Ramón Jiménez, particularly to the latter.[7] In their esthetic direction, their tone and intensity, their delicate imagery, many of the poems of Torres Bodet, Xavier Villaurrutia, and José Gorostiza—to mention only the more obvious examples—show much more than a casual relationship to Jiménez.

"The pine groves" ("pinares"), "the clear water" ("agua limpia"), "the golden sky" ("cielo de oro"), "the sound of flutes"

("son de flautas"), "the soul (which) weeps with the moon" ("el
alma llora con la luna), "the fresh song of the river" ("el canto
fresco del río") could easily be taken for images from Jiménez' *Sad
Airs* or *Pastorals,* but they are from the early poems of Torres
Bodet. In Villaurrutia also, occasional passages attest to his af-
filiation with Jimenez.[8] The following lines, to cite an example,
could easily be mistaken for a quotation from *Summer* or *Eternities:* "How speechless was our passion! / Our silence, how it
burned!" ("¡Cómo callaba nuestro afán! / Nuestra paz ¡cómo
ardía!").[9] In José Gorostiza's *Canciones para cantar en las barcas*
(*Songs to Sing in the Boats*), the delicate imagery, the melodious
verse and the subtle melancholy tone often remind one of the
Jiménez of *Distant Gardens* or *Ballads of Spring.* "Autumn all
nakedness of gold" (Otoño todo desnudez de oro"), the refrain
which runs through Gorostiza's poem "Otoño" ("Autumn"),[10]
unmistakably points to antecedents in the poetry of Jiménez. In
Octavio Paz, a lineal descendant of the "Contemporaries" and
today one of Spanish America's most distinguished poets and
critics, there is abundant evidence that the poetic legacy of Jiménez
has been preserved and respected.[11] One of Paz' early poems expresses this esthetic credo, essentially an invocation and an
exaltation of the "exact word" (*voz exacta*),[12] thus reaffirming
what Jiménez had already set forth in one of his best-known and
most frequently quoted poems.[13] In the same poem Paz further
identifies his esthetic posture with that of Jiménez in the conception
of poetry as the "ineffable" word.[14]

In Peru, Chile, Argentina and all the other countries of Spanish
America there were admirers, and in varying degrees, followers of
Jiménez. Just as in an earlier period every Spanish-American poet
had read and assimilated, consciously or unconsciously, the poetry
and the poetics of Rubén Darío, so in Jiménez' day, and somewhat
later, in Neruda's, most were, at one time or another, drawn into
the orbit of one or another of these two ascendant poets.[15]

II   *Jiménez in the United States*

Before Jiménez came to Miami[16] he had paid two rather brief
visits to the United States, the one in 1916 when he came to be

married to Zenobia, the other in 1936 as a cultural emissary of the ill-fated Azaña government. It was quite a different matter to begin a new life at the age of fifty-eight in a society with which he was only superficially acquainted. His adjustment to the American milieu was, of course, greatly facilitated by having Zenobia, literally, at his side, to concern herself with all irksome, practical details and eliminate certain psychological hazards, of which there were not a few. The poet's deficient English always stood in the way of communication with people in the new environment, but Zenobia was an extraordinary interpreter who translated rapidly and accurately, shifting from Spanish to English, or English to Spanish with amazing facility.

At the time of his arrival in Miami Jiménez was little known outside of academic circles in the United States, and it was not until he won the Nobel Prize in 1956 that he attracted wide attention in this country.[17] It was an American Hispanist, Professor J. Riis Owre, who made arrangements for Jiménez to give lectures on literature at the University of Miami, thus introducing him to the American academic world. Later he lectured at Duke University, at the University of Maryland, and finally at the University of Puerto Rico. Owre, a sensible and sensitive man, understood the poet and helped him become adjusted to life in the American community. Theirs was a cordial friendship that lasted throughout the rest of Jiménez' life.

After becoming established in an apartment in the suburb of Coral Gables, not far from the University of Miami, the poet resumed his work. One of his collections of poems, *Romances de Coral Gables* (*Ballads of Coral Gables*),[18] is only a small part of what he wrote in Florida. During the three years he spent there, he continued the flow of letters, poems and articles for publication in the literary journals of Spanish America.

In the United States 1942 was a year of much public anxiety over the war, but it produced enthusiastic support of the cause of the allied nations. Jiménez demonstrated his concern and his solidarity with that cause by moving to Washington and offering his services to the State Department. He was involved for a time in the organization of cultural programs to be broadcast to Latin America, part of a broader effort by the coordinator of Latin American Affairs to solicit the moral and material support of the other nations of the Western Hemisphere.[19] However, the poet's decision to establish his residence in Washington may have been prompted by his own restlessness quite as much as by his feeling of loyalty to the country in which he had found refuge.

In Washington Jiménez and his wife had a large apartment on one of the tree-lined streets not far from the Capitol. Writers, artists and diplomats from all the Latin-American countries sought interviews with the poet. Not all were admitted, but often he was surrounded by visitors and admirers whom Zenobia had not seen fit to turn away. Jiménez also had a number of friends and acquaintances among American writers. John Gould Fletcher, Herschel Brickell, Muna Lee and William Dudley Poore were among those he found congenial. He also saw something of Ezra Pound after the American poet's involuntary return to the United States from Italy, accused of collaboration with the Fascist regime during World War II. To Pound he once remarked, "I am an exile *from* my country, and you are an exile *in* your country". Henry Wallace, then vice president of the United States, was another frequent visitor. Wallace, intent on learning Spanish, used to come to the Jiménez' apartment carrying a Spanish book—often a volume of verse by the poet himself—and a small notebook in which he would often jot down some thought, or a comment made by the poet. The conversations were friendly and animated, on a variety of subjects.[20]

The change of scene from Spain to America did not prove to be the creative stimulant it had been in 1916, the year Jiménez "discovered" America. After that memorable voyage he published five books of poetry in rather close succession, but the initial three years spent in Puerto Rico and Cuba were rather barren so far as his poetic production was concerned. At a later date he said he wrote almost exclusively in prose during those years and that it was not until after he moved to Florida that he began to write in verse again.[21] There is little question that from his thirty-fifth to his forty-second year (1916 to 1923) he wrote more poetry of significance than during any other comparable period of his life. In 1944 a new edition of his "second" anthology was published in Buenos Aires, but all that was new in it was the paper on which it was printed; the content was exactly the same as that of the edition of 1922, printed in Madrid. Another book of poems, *Voces de mi copla* (*Voices of My Song*),[22] is a collection of eighty-five short lyrics, grouped under several new subtitles, but every one of them had appeared earlier in

Song.[23] Jiménez may have assumed that he was now addressing a different reading public, no longer that of Spain but of America, and that his old poems would be new to many of his readers in America.

III   Total Season *and* Ballads of Coral Gables

Two significant books of verse appeared before the Jiménez made their trip to Argentina and Uruguay in 1948, *Estación total (Total Season)*[24] and *Romances de Coral Gables (Ballads of Coral Gables).*[25] In *Total Season* Jiménez again published a collection of his earlier compositions, but this time added many poems never included in any previous volume.[26] Apparently it was his intention that *Total Season* be a distillation of all his poetic experience and an affirmation of the esthetic and spiritual values of his maturity. It is at once a summation of his earlier work and a link between the *Diary*—the book which marks the beginning of the poet's quest for a more transcendent reality than temporal beauty and love—and *Animal de fondo (Animal of Depth)*—the book of exultation and fulfillment. *Total Season* is thus a key book—as Guillermo Díaz Plaja has accurately stated[27] in Jiménez' poetic evolution.

The tension which is released in poetic creation is in most cases generated by a duality in the poet's psyche, and concomitantly, in his outlook on life. In the books which immediately precede *Total Season* there is a pervasive aspiration to attain a wholeness of being, the true fulfillment of the poet's destiny. However, his life holds no *promise* of fulfillment, only hints of its possibility, for the present is "neither light nor shadow / neither truth nor untruth" (LP, 1047). Jiménez is alternately sustained by hope and tormented by doubt. In one of the numerous poems which clearly have their origin in this dichotomy he speaks of "my half of light", and "my half of shadow" (LP, 1116). Only the final union of the two will complete his being. In the poem he addresses death directly. Thus it is evident—in this instance, at least—that he sees death as the only possible consummation of his wholeness, the union of his "day being" and his "night being".

It is somewhat surprising, then, that *Total Season* should begin with a poem so confident and positive in tone as "Desde dentro"

("From Within"). The opening line—"My soul broke through with gold" ("Rompió mi alma con oro")[28]—appears to announce an unusual and exalted experience, a sublime discovery or revelation. Unlike most of Jiménez' poems, there is in this one almost no mention of nature. It is of an imminent discovery that he speaks, of inner, not outer vision. The poet's "revelation" parallels very closely the experience of Plotinus, who spoke of "becoming external to all other beings and self-centered; beholding a marvelous beauty...acquiring identity with the divine".[29] The divinity thus revealed to Jiménez is that of poetry and love, both spelled with capital letters in the poem, a significant detail. His encounter with Poetry and Love in the center of his being has the impact of a religious conversion:

> Since then, what peace!
> no longer I stretch my hands
> outward. The infinite
> is within me. I am
> the horizon gathered in.
>
> She, Poetry, Love, the center
> beyond doubt.
>
> Desde entonces ¡que paz!
> no tiendo ya hacia fuera
> mis manos. Lo infinito
> está dentro. Yo soy
> el horizonte recojido.
>
> Ella, Poesía, Amor, el centro
> indudable.

(LP, 1135, *Total Season*)

The poet's discovery of the infinite within himself is a recurring theme in *Total Season* and gives the individual poems their continuity and the book its unity. What has seemed to be an obsessive preoccupation with self has led some readers and critics to speak with something short of praise of Jiménez' narcissism.[30] The criticism is understandable and in some ways justifiable, particularly at a time when many consider the function of art to be solely service to society, and when there is some tendency to discredit its purely subjective forms. Many of Jiménez' poems would thus seem to be outmoded or "irrelevant", to use one of the favorite clichés of the day. Yet there is a marked difference between the morbid self-absorption of many poems of earlier collections and the mature serenity of *Total Season*. The egocentricity has not disappeared but it is more dignified than its rather childish and petulant manifestations in earlier poems.

In the poems which follow "From Within" it becomes evident, further, that the poet's ecstatic inner vision is not what would normally be identified as that of a religious mystic, although they may nearly coincide in their elevation and intensity.[31] What seems to have been latent in his psyche since his early years has at last reached its time of fruition: a total awareness—and this is his exultant discovery—of the beauty and harmony of the universe, which would have no reality or existence except as perceived and recreated through this awareness. The poet experiences a total harmony, in which he not only identifies himself with nature, but also transcends it. The first stanza of "El otoñado" expresses the new "reality" of the poet's existence:

> I am complete with nature,
> in the full afternoon of golden maturity,
> high wind through the verdure.
> Rich, hidden fruit, I contain
> the elemental great within me (earth,
> fire, water, air) infinity.

> Estoy completo de naturaleza,
> en plena tarde de áurea madurez,
> alto viento en lo verde traspasado.
> Rico fruto recóndito, contengo
> lo grande elemental en mí (la tierra,
> el fuego, el agua, el aire) el infinito.

(LP, 1140)

In *Total Season* the poet attains a maturity which Luis Vivanco terms "the plenitude of the real".[32] In no previous work has Jiménez used the word plenitude so insistently. Round (*redondo*) and its corresponding noun roundness (*redondez*) also occur with frequency, for they connote fulfillment, completeness, plenitude.

The poet's vision had until the present enabled him only fleetingly and imperfectly to glimpse or sense a more transcendent reality than the one he perceived with his senses.

"Plenitude", which would be an appropriate title for the whole collection, is that of only one poem (LP, 1146-1147). However, this poem might well serve as an exegesis for the entire book. Now, at last, the poet is conscious of a plenitude of three dimensions: the "eternal plenitude", revealed through nature; the "external plenitude", revealed through the senses; the "inner plenitude", the discovery of the inner "reality", perhaps intuition of that imminent god of which he later speaks in *Animal of Depth*. It is significant that in each instance the adjective "naked" modifies "plenitude" and that in several other poems of *Total Season* it is repeated almost to the point of monotony. In earlier works it had usually had an esthetic connotation, particularly with reference to poetry. "Naked" poetry was to Jiménez what some would have called "pure" poetry. However, it is evident that in *Total Season* the word embraces more than esthetic criteria. Nature is "naked" in its freedom from embellishment, sentimentality and didacticism; the poet's inner plenitude is free of ennui, anxiety and doubt;[33] the eternal plenitude is a direct vision or intuition of eternity, unobscured by superstition or tradition, or by philosophical and theological fog. "Plenitude" and several other poems[34] of the collection are testimony of the "harmony without end" ("Armonía sin fin"), attained or near attainment. Of this harmony is born the serenity and the ecstasy which pervade the first and the third "cantos" of *Total Season*. The interpolated poems taken from *Song* form an interlude, "Songs of the New Light" ("Canciones de la nueva luz"), which varies rather than sustains the tone of parts one and three.

There is, of course, a problem in communicating to others an intensely subjective experience or verity wholly through the medium of the printed word. Partial or total obscurity can result. Ambiguity is inevitable and, as Octavio Paz has pointed out, it is even necessary in a poem if it is to avoid the rigidity which fetters the imagination instead of liberating it.[35] The poem may have as many different meanings as it has readers. Vivanco considers *Total Season* and *Animal of Depth*—about which more will be said presently—to be the expression of a sincere religious experience, yet he is careful to point out that this has nothing to do with the personal transcendent God of Christianity or other monotheistic religions.[36] Osvaldo Lira differs notably from Vivanco in his view that the identification of the internal with the eternal, as it is revealed in *Total Season,* is the work of God. It is God, says Lira, who directs the poet's vision inward to discover the work that He is performing in the poet's soul.[37] Perhaps Jiménez position is somewhere between these two extremes. Nowhere in *Total Season* does he mention God, but nature, beauty, love, poetry, grace all converge in the total awareness which the poet experiences in the "undoubted center". "Mensajera de la estación total" ("The messenger of the total season"), the final poem, is the confirmation and the affirmation of the "plenitude of the real", the inner radiance of the poet's spirit merging with the outer radiance of nature (water, fire, earth, air) and the universe in the glorious harmony of the totality. The "messenger", as if in fulfillment of a prophesy, "...was coming, and was coming" ("venía y venía"), an allusion perhaps to those moments in the past when the poet had fleeting glimpses or sensed intuitively the possibility of the "total season". The "messenger" is the embodiment of all matter and spirit, the external as well as the internal, that brought the poet to this culminating experience.[38] That he intended to project this experience beyond the egocentric to the universal is evident from one of the closing stanzas of the poem:

> (Messenger,
> what glory to see in order to see oneself,
> in oneself,
> in one himself,
> in one herself,
> the glory which comes from us!)

> (Mensajera
> ¡qué gloria ver para verse a sí mismo,
> en sí mismo,
> en uno mismo,
> en una misma,
> la gloria que proviene de nosotros!)

(LP, 1283)

The pronouns "oneself", "himself", "herself", "us", rather

than "myself" and "me", indicate that Jiménez meant to com-
municate his exalted discovery to others and perhaps to suggest to
them that they look inward to find the imminent glory or divinity
of which they may not be aware. The stanza is not an example of
Jiménez' best poetry, but it reiterates and in a sense confirms what
the initial poem had stated. The glory of which the poet speaks here
is again reminiscent of Plotinus' experience of the divine. But
whatever may have led Jiménez to his own experience of the divine,
to total awareness of the outer beauty and light and that which
emanated from within, this experience is the substance of *Total
Season*, in which a new note is heard in his poetry.

Total Season uses a variety of verse forms, generally unrhymed,
but *Ballads of Coral Gables* is made up exclusively of the octosyllabic *verso de romance,* most often with assonance occurring
in the even-numbered lines of the twenty poems of the collection.
As accurately as can be determined, all the poems were written in
Coral Gables between 1939 and 1942. The white houses, the
sunlight, sea and pines of this region reminded Jiménez of his
native Moguer, as he remarked on more than one occasion.
However, except for an occasional concrete image in the *Ballads*
there is nothing that suggests any particular locale. The images in
general tend toward the abstract and the symbolic rather than the
descriptive. There is no unifying theme, if there is any at all. The
Ballads, like the principle poems of *Total Season*, are the expression of a metaphysical preoccupation, sometimes positive in
tone, sometimes negative. From the aura of fulfillment that
characterizes *Total Season,* Jiménez reverts to the disquietude and
the restless seeking that was the source of so many of his earlier
poems. The poet's spirit is like a flame now burning serenely, again
flickering fitfully in the wind of doubt. The second and third poems
of the *Ballads* exemplify the two moods.

But the Only Thing

The palm tree caresses the pine
with this air of water;
in the other, the pine, the pine
caressed the palm tree.

And the blue and green night

is a green and violet night,
the moon almost shows me
hope in its mirror.

But the only thing is here,
but faith does not change,
but what was without,
now is only within my soul.

Pero lo solo

La palma acaricia al pino
con este aire de agua;
en aquel, el pino, el pino
acariciaba a la palma.

Y la noche azul y verde
es noche verde y morada,
la luna casi me enseña
en su espejo la esperanza.

Pero lo solo está aquí
pero la fe no se cambia
pero lo que estaba fuera,
ahora está solo en el alma.

(*Ballads of Coral Gables,* p. 13)[39]

What is typical of these *Ballads* is the simplicity of the language and the complexity of the sentiment; typical also is the pleasing nature imagery, which in this poem links the present emotionally with a specific time in the past ("the other"), just as it will later in *Animal of Depth.* The regularity of the form does not constrain the spontaneity of expression. The identical assonance (a—a) in all the even-numbered lines (*agua, palma, morada,* etc.) sustains the simple melody and links each stanza to the one that follows. The introspective climax of the closing stanza seems to confirm what Jiménez had exultantly announced in *Total Season.*

"Con tu piedra" ("With Your Stone") is the title of the next poem. Only in its octosyllabic form, and the assonance (e—a), maintained in the even lines, is it similar to the preceding one. The first stanza, quoted below, will serve to illustrate the difference:

With Your Stone

The sky has the weight
of a quarry of stone.
Above the stone of the world
is the stone of the stars.

El cielo pesa lo mismo
que una cantera de piedra.
Sobre la piedra del mundo
son de piedra las estrellas.

(*Ballads,* 14-15)

The stanzas which follow are repetitious and monotonous, as
some of Jiménez' poems are in their insistence on one note, one
chromatic effect or mood. (This has already been noted in Chapter
3.) In this shift from the transparent imagery of the preceding poem
to the opaqueness of "With Your Stone" one is reminded of the
dichotomy suggested by the title of one of Jiménez' earlier books,
Rock and Sky. In his quest of the absolute, Jiménez' metaphoric
trajectory is one of space, movement and light. The world of stone
and the stars of stone are their negation, symbols of total despair.

However, despair is not the prevailing sentiment of the *Ballads.*
There is a resurgence of the poet's aspiration to transcend the
sensible world, the known and the unknown, the temporal and the
eternal. Several of the succeeding poems of *Ballads* are the expression of this "passion for transcendence", as Paul Olson has
called it.[40] "Más allá que yo", ("Beyond Me"), quoted in part
below, is an example·

Beyond, and ever beyond,
beyond all the earth
and all the sky and sea?...

Beyond me in nothingness,
me in my nothingness, beyond
nothingness itself, beyond all being
now without me, still beyond? [41]

...¿Más allá, más, más allá,

allá que toda la tierra,
todo el cielo y todo el mar?

¿Más allá que yo en la nada,
más que yo en mi nada, más
que la nada y más que el todo
ya sin mí, más, más allá?

(Ballads, 20-21)

"Pinar de la eternidad" ("Pine Grove of Eternity") is the title of another poem engendered by the same passion but which, like many of the poems of *Total Season,* also embraces a vision of fulfillment of the poet's aspiration. Nature is as usual the source of the imagery; and it is again identified with that "plenitude of the real" the poet has sought. The temporal pine trees, which the poet loved, will, like him, be transported and reappear in the realm of ideal fulfillment in eternity. In the first stanza the poet envisions that the pines will be present when he embarks on his transcendent journey—"...through these pines I shall go / to an eternal pine that is waiting" ("por estos pinos iré / a un pino eterno que espera...")—and, in the closing stanza, that he will see pines, firm and sonorous in the primordial sand of that eternal shore where "with full soul" he will arrive. It has been noted already that Jiménez retained, perhaps unconsciously, some of the religious beliefs of his childhood. That he hoped for eternal life in a more traditional sense than he sometimes admitted is evident from some of the things he said and wrote. It is possible that the eternity of his poem is only an abstraction, and that its pines are only ambiguous symbols, but it is also possible that Jiménez saw eternity in another light, and that, as he conceived it, or hoped it would be, there would be pines, eternal in their greenness, strength and beauty. One must concede to such a vision of eternity some superiority over one of a city whose streets are paved with gold, particularly in the case of a man who loved nature intensely, as Jiménez did.

Another poem, "Arboles hombres" ("Tree Men"), is charming in its whimsy, simplicity and beauty. In it too the poet identifies himself closely with nature, standing motionless among the trees to listen to their conversation, and finally leaving them regretfully, not wishing to deceive them into thinking he is one of them. Much

of the appeal of the poem lies in the ingenuous personification of
the trees and the poet's sensitivity to their "feelings". Two stanzas
are quoted below:

> And I listened to them talk,
> amid the pearly clouds,
> with soft voices, about me.
> And how could I undeceive them?
>
> How could I tell them no,
> that I was only a passer-by,
> that they shouldn't speak to me?
> I didn't want to betray them....
>
> Y yo los oía hablar,
> entre el nublado de nácares,
> con blando rumor, de mí.
> Y ¿cómo desengañarles?
>
> ¿Cómo decirles que no,
> que yo era sólo el pasante,
> que no me hablaran a mí?
> No quería traicionarles.... [42]

(Ballads, 40)

The *Ballads* end with a poem which expresses with greater intensity than any other in the collection the poet's ardent yearning
for the absolute in beauty, purity, freedom, imperishability,
totality. The central image, reminiscent of Blake, is that of an
ember flaming eternally, never to be consumed. It is the poet's
supreme aspiration to attain this eternal radiance in his own being:

> Incandescent blood and flame
> white and blue, where all
> would be transfigured, content
> to be the faithful fuel. ...
>
> Sangre incandescente y llama
> blanca y azul, donde insigne
> se hiciera todo, contento
> de ser el fiel combustible. ...

(Ballads, 55)

IV   Espacio (Space)

Another work which was a distillation of Jiménez' Florida experience and was at least partially composed there is the long poem, or prose poem as it has also been called, *Espacio* (*Space*). The first part of *Space* was published in the well-known Mexican journal *Cuadernos Americanos* in 1943, the second in the same magazine in 1944, both in free verse. Both were republished in 1954, together with part three, all in prose, in the magazine *Poesía Española* of Madrid.[43] Formally at least, *Space* is a marked departure from the type of poetry Jiménez had written all his life. Until he wrote *Space* he had accepted the Symbolist tenet, derived from Poe, that "a long poem does not exist".[44] However, by 1940 there were already many precedents in contemporary literature that may have influenced Jiménez in his deviation from the short, intense lyric which he had always preferred until then. Graciela Nemes notes that after the publication of the first part of *Space* critics compared Jiménez with T. S. Eliot, whose *The Waste Land* appeared in 1922.[45] Except for some similarities in structure, the resemblance is not notable. Even fewer points of comparison could be found with Pound's *Cantos*, most of which were published in the thirties.[46] If Jiménez had needed examples to follow, he could easily have found them in contemporary Hispanic literature in such poets as Unamuno of Spain, Vicente Huidobro and Pablo Neruda of Chile, José Gorostiza of Mexico.[47] However, *Space* does not closely resemble the long poetic compositions of any of these authors, and probably owes nothing to any of them except, indirectly to Unamuno.[48]

Space is a long poem made up of three "fragments", as the author called them, each a sort of soliloquy not consciously developed around any central theme, but rather the expression of a succession of poetic impulses between which there is often no apparent, logical link. All are part of the same flow of consciousness. There is something in this creative process which resembles the automatism of the Surrealists but it cannot properly be called Surrealism. There is no reason to suspect that this long, rambling poem meant the abandonment of the esthetic principle

Jiménez had always followed in his poetry, "the spontaneous subjected to the conscious" ("lo espontáneo sometido a lo consciente"). There is throughout *Space* a metaphysical train of thought—interrogation more than affirmation—hardly consonant with the tenets of the Surrealists, who held that the intellect was extraneous to poetic creation. The imagery of *Space* is not an exhibit of the dredgings of the subconscious but a recreation of the real—sea, wind, sky, trees, flowers, birds, colors, light, sound —just as in his other works.

The poem begins with an ontological inquiry in which both intellect and emotion are involved:

The gods had no more substance than that which I have. I have, like them, the substance of everything to be lived. I am not present only, but an impetuous flight from beginning to end. And what I see on one side and the other in this flight (roses, remnants of wings, shadow, light) is mine alone, memory and longing of mine, presentiment, oblivion. Who knows more than I, who, what man or god can, has been able, will be able to tell me what my life and my death are, what they are not? If there is anyone who knows it, I know it more than he, and anyone who is ignorant of it, I am more ignorant of it than he. A struggle between this not knowing and this knowing is my life, his life, and it is life. Winds go by like birds, birds like flowers, flowers suns and moons, moon suns like me, like souls, like bodies, bodies like death and resurrection; like gods. I am a god without sword, without anything that men make with their science; only with what is the product of what lives, what changes wholly; yes, of fire or of light, light. Why do we eat and drink anything but light or fire? Since I was born in the sun, and from the sun I have come here to the shadow, am I of sun, do I give light like the sun?, and my nostalgia, like that of the moon is having been sun of a sun one day and now reflecting it only.... [49]

The first impression of this passage may be somewhat bewildering, particularly to readers familiar with Jiménez' more typical works. However, the emotional impulse is the same as that which produced all the works of Jiménez' so-called "second" period: the *Diary, Eternities, Beauty,* etc. This is the nostalgia which the poet compares to that of the moon, the homesickness for the realm of light from which he came and to which he is to return. *Space* is more rambling and diffuse than the earlier poems but also more varied; it comprises not only lyric, but also descriptive, narrative, metaphysical elements. In the first and third "fragments" there are repeated references to Coral Gables, and to

Florida. Anyone familiar with that region will note the realism of some of the imagery in the poem: the live oak trees, gnarled, hollow, broken, with their streamers of Spanish moss like funereal veils; the heavy scent of orange blossoms; the mangrove swamps, their flora and faun and among the latter, particularly the land crab—real and symbolic—of the third fragment. But all this is secondary to the vision of a paradise in which the poet is enraptured by the song of the birds, the light, the trees with their fruits, their rhythm, their grace and their subtle strength. "Is this to live?" the poet asks. "Is there anything more than this living of change and glory? Always I hear that music which sounds in the depth of everything, farther on; it is what calls me from the sea, in the street, in my sleep" (TA, 854). The song of the nightingale is only the "demeaned prologue" of that other mysterious and more exalted music. [50]

Space expresses with beauty and intensity the yearning for transcendence which dominates the poet's life, but it is also a song of human love, love of woman; it eulogizes Héloise, the epitome of ideal love, and it censures Abelard for falsifying that love. Man fares rather badly: "...no, I want nothing to do with man; he is stupid, unfaithful, mistrustful; and when he is most fawning, scientific". This is one of the discordant notes in this symphony of light, beauty and song, but the disruption is only momentary. "Supreme is life, supreme, and sweet. Sweet like this light was love; how placid also this love." The allusion here is plainly to two different loves, and it is pertinent to point out that Jiménez was not in love with abstractions but with women of flesh and blood. The first fragment ends with an outpouring of amorous sentiment. The enamored poet listens in rapture to the song of the bird, the perfect expression of his love: "...how I adore you, eternal brother, bird of grace and glory, humble, delicate, free; angel of our air, lavisher of complete music. Bird, I love you as I love the woman, your sister more than mine" (TA, 861).

As in hundreds of other poems by Jiménez, nature and love are the source and sustenance of *Space,* but Florida brought him a *new* experience of nature. The landscape itself, unbroken by mountains, hills or gorges, overwhelmed him with a sensation of unlimited space, and it was this sensation which dictated the poem and determined the freedom of its form. [51] Toward the end of the first fragment the poet exults, "Immensity, in you and now I

live....Space and time and light I in everything, in all...." It is as if
the limits of space and time had been obliterated, their barriers
surmounted.[52] Thus there is in the poem a strange juxtaposition of
past and present and of places widely separated; the oak trees of
Florida merge with the pines of Moguer, the white herons of one
place with those of the other; a dog barks in Coral Gables but the
poet hears him in the Moguer of his childhood. Places lose their
identity: New York is the same as Moguer, Seville or Madrid. Had
Jiménez never seen Florida, it is reasonably certain *Space* would
never have been written. *Space* is a spontaneous flow of fantasy
and reminiscence interspersed with metaphysical inquiry, ecstatic
contemplation of nature, the expression of the exhilaration of love.
It is not the most perfect of Jiménez' poems but one of the most
original of them. Despite its deviations from the norm, it maintains
the essential unity of the poet's total work.

The exact date of composition of the third fragment is not
known but it is one of Jiménez' latest poems, possibly as much as
five years later than *Animal of Depth*. It may have been begun,
after the completion of the other two fragments, when the poet still
lived in Coral Gables, but the final version is certainly later by at
least ten years than the date of Jiménez' definitive departure from
Florida. In the poet's retrospective vision it is Florida and Spain,
Miami and Moguer, which reappear most insistently. The "Third
Fragment" is filled with allusions to the two regions, which merge
in space and time in his stream of consciousness. The ontological
questions which—as we shall see in part V of this chapter—were
resolved in *Animal of Depth* are raised again in the third fragment,
and the closing lines of the poem are charged with the anxiety of a
man who speaks for all men as he asks whether the dissolution of
his physical being will also mean the end of consciousness, or as he
puts it, the incorporation of his god with another being to become
another god.

V   *Animal of Depth*

Animal of Depth (*Animal de fondo*), published in 1949, very
shortly after the Jiménez returned from a triumphant lecture tour
of Argentina and Uruguay, was at least partially composed on

board the Rio Juramento, the ship on which they traveled to those countries.[52] The book was intended to be the first part of a more extensive work to be called *Dios deseado y deseante* (*God Desired and Desiring*), which was begun but never completed.

The twenty-nine poems which made up *Animal of Depth* are not like the individual poems in other collections by Jiménez, but in their unity and continuity they are links in a single prosodic chain. The poems were all born of the same impulse, and each serves as a conductor through which the current of emotion flows uninterrupted through the entire sequence. A number of critics have commented on the dynamic character of the rhythm which they liken to the movement of the sea, suggesting that the measured rising and falling of the boat on the waves is consciously reproduced in the rhythmic pattern of the verse.[54] There are, in effect, many references in the poems to the gentle rocking of the sea. Again the soothing physical sensation, not unlike that felt by a child rocked in its mother's arms, contributes to an unusual buoyancy of spirit which animates the poet throughout the creation of *Animal of Depth*. Only one previous work, *Total Season,* anticipates the exalted sense of fulfillment which Jiménez experiences in *Animal of Depth*. Doubt no longer afflicts him. He is sustained by the conviction that he has at last attained what he had sought ever since childhood. *Animal of Depth* is a joyous song of triumph. There is not a note of sadness or despair in any of the poems. The poet is like one who exults that a summit has been reached after a long and arduous upward journey.[55] It is as if Jiménez now viewed all his previous work as preparation for a definitive work, to be the culmination of his creative experience. In the notes appended to the poems he attempts an elucidation of his position:

I wrote these poems while I thought, now in this lateness of my life,...about what I had done in this world to find a possible god through poetry. And I thought then that the way toward a god was the same as any way to a calling, mine as a poetic writer, in this case; that all my poetic progress was a progress toward god, because I was creating a world the end of which was to be a god. ...

Estos poemas los escribí yo mientras pensaba, ya en estas penúltimas de mi vida,...en lo que había yo hecho en este mundo para encontrar un dios posible por la poesía. Y pensé entonces que el camino hacia un dios era el

mismo que cualquier camino vocativo, el mío de escritor poético, en este
case; que todo mi avance poético en la poesía era avance hacia dios, porque
estaba creando un mundo del cual había de ser el fin un dios. ... [56]

It is evident from these comments that Jiménez meant *Animal of
Depth* to be a summation of his life's work as a poet, viewing that
work as now nearly completed. In the notes, and in the poems, he
often uses religious metaphors, reversing the procedure of San
Juan de la Cruz, who wrote of divine love in the language of human
love. In *Animal of Depth* Jiménez does not humanize the divine but
confers divinity on the human; he deifies his own sensibility. Yet,
the poetic experience, he affirms, is a religious experience. To
reiterate what was stated earlier, Jiménez' readers and critics often
speak of his "mysticism", a term which requires ample
qualification if applied to *Animal of Depth*. The first poem of the
twenty-nine, "La transparencia, dios, la transparencia",
"Transparency, God, Transparency", identifies the god with
whom the poet is in intimate communion, not as God the Creator,
not as the omnipotent Lord of the universe, not as Father, Son or
Holy Ghost but as the poet's awareness of the beautiful, a god, but
not God in the usual sense:

> God of the coming, I feel you in my hands,
> here you are engaged with me in a beautiful struggle
> of love, the same
> as fire with its air.
>
> You are not my redeemer, nor are you my example,
> nor my father, nor my son, nor my brother;
> you are the same and one, you are different and all;
> you are the god of beauty attained,
> my awareness of the beautiful...
>
> Dios del venir, te siento entre mis manos,
> aquí estás enredado conmigo, en lucha hermosa
> de amor, lo mismo
> que un fuego con su aire.
>
> No eres mi redentor, ni eres mi ejemplo,
> ni mi padre, ni mi hijo, ni mi hermano;
> eres igual y uno; eres distinto y todo;

eres dios de lo hermoso conseguido,
conciencia mía de lo hermoso...

(LP, 1289)

The theme of this introductory poem is actually that of the entire
series, the jubilant meeting of the poet with his god, each having
long sought the other. The imagery of the first stanza is striking
and effective. The meeting is a personal encounter in which the
poet wrestles with his god, much as Jacob wrestled with God in the
book of Genesis, both contending, not through enmity, but love.
The ardor of the sentiment—as Ricardo Gullón has pointed
out [57]—could not be captured more intensely than in the simile "the
same / as a fire with its air". However, the ambiguity of the book
begins with the second stanza, which disclaims any identity between
the poet's god and the God of the Old Testament or of the New.
The last two verses of the stanza speak more of an esthetic than a
religious experience. As the poem develops it appears that both love
and beauty are attributes of this elusive deity. The succeeding
stanzas of the poem illustrate the complexity of *Animal of Depth*,
for they amplify the poet's conception of his god, just as the
succeeding poems do, sometimes in paradoxical or contradictory
terms. The god who appears in the initial poem is "essence",
"awareness" ("conciencia"), "grace" and all that these imply, as
the final stanza indicates:

> You are the free grace,
> the glory of enjoyment, the eternal attraction,
> the thrill of the tremor, the light
> of clairvoyance, the depth of love,
> the horizon which conceals nothing;
> transparency, god, transparency,
> the one at last, god now at home in my oneness,
> in the world which I because of you and for you have created.

> Eres la gracia libre,
> la gloria del gustar, la eterna simpatía,
> el gozo del temblor, la luminaria
> del clariver, el fondo del amor,
> el horizonte que no quita nada;

la trasparencia, dios, la trasparencia,
el uno al fin, dios ahora sólito en lo uno mío,
en el mundo que yo por ti y para ti he creado.

(LP, 1290)

Transparency, with its connotation of limpidity, clarity, purity,
may refer to the esthetic ideal which the poet had long pursued and
at last attained, but also to the perception of verities which until the
present had remained undiscovered. The word *clariver* [58]suggests
the latter meaning, which is supported further by the verse "the
horizon which conceals nothing". The horizon which normally is
the limit of our vision, and beyond which we can only conjecture
what may exist, now permits the poet to see what he had heretofore
only vaguely sensed. This is the transcendence he had so ardently
sought. That the poem is concerned with poetry itself and the
creative process is clearly established in the two concluding verses.
The world which the poet has created because of his god and for his
god is that of poetry. It is here that the joyous meeting of the poet
and his god takes place. These two verses conclude the first poem
and introduce the theme of the second. The content of the latter is
summarized in one brief stanza, the penultimate of the poem, in
which the poet again speaks of creating poetry, or recreating the
universe through the power of the poetic word, the god of poetry:

All the names I gave
the universe which for your sake I recreated,
are changing into one and into
a god.

Todos los nombres que yo puse
al universo que por ti me recreaba yo,
se me están convirtiendo en uno y en un
dios.

(LP, 1292)

Awesome, dynamic and beautiful, the sea impressed Jiménez
more powerfully than any other aspect of nature. Both the *Diary*
and *Animal of Depth* were written under its spell. In the loneliness

of the sea, as well as among men, he is aware of the presence of his god of beauty and of poetry. The third poem of *Animal of Depth* begins with this affirmation: "You are not only among men, / desired god; you are here also in this sea.../ Here you form yourself with permanent / movement of lights and colors" (LP, 1293). The movement, the lights and colors of the sea reveal the presence of the "desired god". In this poem the god assumes another attribute, that of totality or omnipresence, in "water, air, high fire / with the earth secure in all the horizon". Sea, sky, sun, the distant land —the four elements make up the universe of the poet and his god.

The fourth poem "En mi tercero mar" ("On My Third Sea")[59] again identifies the poet's god with love "in fire, water, earth and air", hence universal love, but not solely spiritual or divine love; his god is also a god of human love, explicitly in a physical sense: "love in my man-body and in the body of woman" ("amor en cuerpo mío de hombre and en cuerpo de mujer"), verses which again stress the totality of man's being, the unity of substance and essence. Jiménez' "mysticism" embraces matter as well as spirit, for his god, whom he addresses in the poem, is the god of complete love:

> The most complete love, love, you are,
> with all the substance
> (and with all the essence)
> in the senses of my body
> (and in all the senses of my soul)
> which are the same in the great knowledge
> of him, who like me now, in light, knows all...

> El amor más completo, amor, tú eres,
> con la sustancia toda
> (Y con toda la esencia)
> en los sentidos todos de mi cuerpo
> (Y en todos los sentidos de mi alma)
> que son los mismos en el gran saber
> de quien, como yo ahora, todo, en luz, lo sabe...

(LP, 1296)

There is no mention of knowledge (*saber, sabiduría*) anywhere in *Animal of Depth* except in the poem "On My Third Sea". What, then, is the "great knowledge" to which the poet refers in line six of the stanza quoted? Most plausibly it is the "awareness" of which he first spoke in the opening poem of *Animal of Depth*, and which is actually the central theme of all the poems it contains. This is confirmed in the final stanza of the poem:

> He knows it, for he knew it more and more;
> the more, the more, the only road to knowledge;
> now finally I know I am complete,
> because you, my desired god, are visible,
> you are audible, you are perceptible
> in sound and color of the sea, now;
> because you are the mirror of myself
> in the world—greater because of you—which is my lot.

> Lo sabe, pues lo supo más y más;
> el más, el más, camino único de la sabiduría;
> ahora yo sé ya que soy completo,
> porque tú, mi deseado dios, estás visible,
> estás audible, estás sensible
> en rumor y en color de mar, ahora;
> porque eres espejo de mi mismo
> en el mundo, mayor por ti, que me ha tocado.

(LP, 1296)

The poet now affirms confidently that he is "complete". In nature (the sea) he finds visible and audible evidence of the presence of his "desiring god". Perhaps no poem of *Animal of Depth* exemplifies better the "unifying vision" of which Sanchez Barbudo has spoken,[60] a mystic experience in which the perceiver's identity merges with that of what is perceived. Jiménez' "desiring god" is thus the "mirror" of himself. This is the knowledge he now possesses.

"La fruta de mi flor" ("The Fruit of my Flower") is another poem of exalted consummation, similar to some of those of *Total Season,* but now the imagery becomes more abstract as the poet's vision is directed wholly inward. His awareness of beauty and poetry, which had encircled him like a halo throughout his life, has now entered his own being: "Now the halo is within / and now my body is the visible / center of myself...." The fruit-flower image which first appeared in *Total Season* now reappears, a dual symbol of promise and fulfillment, the beginning of the poetic experience and its maturity, the first intuition of the god of poetry and now the full awareness of his presence, imminent god now at the center of the poet's being: "God, now I am the enclosure of my center, / of you within" (LP, 1300).

From these poems and those which follow there emerges the complex image of a deity who is the god of poetry, of beauty, of nature in all its varied aspects, of love both spiritual and carnal, a god who is present in the universe, among men and in the poet's being. Yet nowhere in *Animal of Depth* is he identified unequivocally as God. The poet's notes which follow the poems may be more effective as obfuscation than clarification. For this reason the opinions of the two critics—both Catholic clergymen—who have given the most attention to the religious aspect of *Animal of Depth* seem of particular relevance. After making a well-documented study of Jiménez' life, his religious training, his literary work and the evolution of his religious thought, Carlos del Saz Orozco is able to list a series of objective conclusions he has reached concerning the poet's concept of God. He characterizes Jiménez' "mysticism" as more sentimental than religious. He notes the poet's total rejection of certain principles of Catholic doctrine, comments on the possible philosophic influences of Nietzsche, Schopenhauer, Loisy, the Krausists and others of the Kantian line, and finally the evolution of a god identified with universal consciousness, the deification of poetry and beauty. This is the imminent god of *Animal of Depth*, but not the Christian God.[61]

Osvaldo Lira, the second of the religious critics, reaches different conclusions concerning Jiménez' concept of God. He sees in the intensity of Jiménez' poetic experience itself an experience of the mystery of God. Concerning *Animal of Depth* he writes:

What informs the last creations of Juan Ramón is now the declared mystic experience. This is revealed especially in *Animal of Depth,* even though the poet may insist absurdly on stressing irreducible differences between his god, written thus, with a small letter, and the true God, much more intimate to his subjectivity than he had imagined; that God in whom *we live, move and have our being....*[62]

After examining the first poem of *Animal of Depth*, Lira makes

several interesting observations, from which the following is
quoted:

> We are not now before beauty, intelligence or eternity, nor before any of
> the diverse abstract or transcendental values in whose contemplation and
> experience the poet had delighted. Now he is concerned with God with all
> his letters; with a God who, in spite of writing his name with a small letter
> in a last display of resistance, will end by taking complete possession of his
> personality. [63]

The divergence of opinion between the two critics is less
significant than the recognition each accords Jiménez as a poet. He
is neither theologian nor philosopher but an exceptional lyric poet.
It is as a lyric poet that posterity will remember him and venerate
him. The lyricism of *Animal of Depth* is achieved through its
metrical flexibility, its novel and often beautiful imagery, the
dynamic and buoyant spirit sustained throughout the work, the joy
with which it communicates the poet's possession of new insight
into the mystery of his own psyche and into the meaning of his
universe in the totality of its four elements with all their splendor
and power. Two complete poems will serve to exemplify the style,
the structure, and the content of the book.

Full Awareness

You bear me, full awareness, desiring god,
throughout the world.
In this third sea,
I almost hear your voice; your voice of the wind
total occupant of the movement;
of the colors, of the lights
eternal and of the sea.

Your voice of white fire
in the totality of the water, the ship, the sky
marking the courses with delight,
tracing for me with splendor my certain orbit
of dark body
with the shining diamond inside.

Conciencia plena

Tú me llevas, conciencia plena, deseante dios,
por todo el mundo.
En este mar tercero,
casi oigo tu voz; tu voz del viento
ocupante total del movimiento;
de los colores, de las luces
eternos y marinos.

Tu voz de fuego blanco
en la totalidad del agua, el barco, el cielo,
lineando las rutas con delicia,
grabándome con fúlgido mi órbita segura
de cuerpo negro
con el diamante lúcido en su dentro.

(LP, 1301)

In this brief poem Jiménez expresses his rapture as he communes directly with his god (or his God?) in what comes close to prayer or adoration. Here his god sustains him wherever he goes, more literally carries him (*me llevas*), a metaphor no doubt inspired by the ship which is, in effect, carrying him over the sea. The act itself implies that he is borne by a force which is superior to his own strength and capabilities. Thus it appears that the sentiment which moved him to write the poem was not one of self-sufficiency bordering on defiance, an attitude he sometimes exhibited, and which precluded his recognition of God or any deity over which he did not exercise some control. Here he hears the voice of his god in the wind and senses his presence in the movement, the colors, the eternal lights (the sun and the stars) and the lights of the sea (the sun and the stars reflected in the sea).

The second stanza of the poem, one of unusual intensity and beauty, is not a conventional stanza but, like the others in *Animal of Depth*, a rhythmic unit within which the individual verses vary in length and are unrhymed. However, it is worth noting that the stanza begins with a verse of seven syllables, and ends with one of eleven syllables, both traditional verses used frequently in similar combination by San Juan de la Cruz. The stanza used in San Juan's "Canciones del alma" also begins with a seven syllable verse and ends with one of eleven. While Jiménez eschews rhyme, in the

second and the two final verses of the stanza he used e—o
assonance (*cielo, negro, dentro*), which corresponds to the rhyme
in the second and two final verses of the "Canciones del alma". It
is possible that in this case Jiménez did not consciously imitate San
Juan de la Cruz, but very likely he had so thoroughly assimilated
the poetry of the mystic that he frequently, even though at times
perhaps unwittingly, followed his example, in versification as well
as in emotive imagery.[64] With respect to the latter, "tu voz de fuego
blanco", perhaps more than any other image in the poem, would
serve to identify Jiménez as of the lineage of San Juan de la Cruz,
whose igneous imagery so effectively conveyed the ardor of his
spirit.

The "nautical" metaphor, another characteristic of *Animal of
Depth*, is also exemplified in "Full Awareness". The poet's destiny
is like the felicitous passage of a ship along its safely plotted course.
In this metaphor there is again the implication that the poets life is
directed by an intelligence and a power not his own. Of course, it is
possible to consider the poem simply as an expression of the
euphoria that possessed the poet, elated in retrospect by his public
exaltation in Buenos Aires, and overwhelmed by the grandeur and
the beauty of the ocean as he traveled over it in comfort, safety and
well-being. There is no reason to believe that such pleasures are
more properly reserved for successful bankers, diplomats and
industrialists than for successful poets. In Jiménez' asceticism there
was room for enjoyment of travel, applause, digestible food and
comfort. Undoubtedly he preferred them to sackcloth, hair shirts
and flagellation. However, "Full Awareness" is much closer to the
assertion of religious faith than to the celebration of the excellence
and the beauty of the material world. The three closing lines of the
poem are notable for the serenity and beauty with which this faith
is expressed, a faith which confidently views both time and eternity,
the "dark body" aware of its mortality but inwardly resplendent,
illumined by the inextinguishable fire of the "shining diamond"
within it. Here, too, San Juan de la Cruz comes to mind.

The second poem is quoted below in its entirety:

With My Half There

My silver here in the south, in this south,
awareness in radiant silver, shimmering

in the limpid morning,
when spring brings my vitals to bloom!

My silver, here, reply to the silver
which dreamed of this silver in the limpid morning
of my silver Moguer,
of my silver Puerto,
of my silver Cádiz,
I sad child daydreaming always
of the ultrasea, with the ultraland, the ultrasky. [65]

And the ultrasky was here
with this land, the ultraland,
this ultrasea, with this sea.
And here, in this ultrasea, my man-self found,
north and south, his fulfilling awareness,
because this he lacked.

And I am glad with full gladness,
with my half there, my there, completing me,
for now I have my totality,
the silver of mine here in the south, in this south.

Con mi mitad allí

¡Mi plata aquí en el sur, en este sur,
conciencia en plata lucidera, palpitando
en la mañana limpia
cuando la primavera saca flor a mis entrañas!

Mi plata, aquí, respuesta de la plata
que soñaba esta plata en la mañana limpia
de mi Moguer de plata,
de mi Puerto de plata,
de mi Cádiz de plata,
niño yo triste soñeando siempre
el ultramar, con la ultratierra, el ultracielo.

Y el ultracielo estaba aquí
con esta tierra, la ultratierra,
este ultramar, con este mar;
y aquí, en este ultramar, mi hombre encontró,
norte y sur, su conciencia plenitente,

porque ésta le faltaba.

Y estoy alegre de alegría llena
con mi mitad allí, mi allí, completándome,
pues que ya tengo mi totalidad,
la plata mía aquí en el sur, en este sur.

(LP, 1329-1330)

This poem is certainly not among the best that Jiménez wrote,[66]
but it illustrates two aspects of *Animal of Depth* not previously
mentioned. One of these is the link it establishes between the poet's
early awareness of beauty, his intuition of divinity, and what he
now sees as his complete identification with them. The "half" in
the title of the poem refers to his childhood and adolescent years
spent in Moguer, Puerto (Puerto de Santa María) and Cádiz, all on
or near the sea, and thus associated with the silvery beauty of the
ocean, which excited in the young Jiménez the thirst for a more
transcendent beauty. On his voyage over the southern Atlantic
("my silver here in the south") the elderly poet's emotion revivifies
his earlier experience of the sea, and the remembered vision of
beauty merges with the present vision of it to form the totality of
which he speaks in the last stanza of the poem. This totality is thus
simultaneously past and present, the only reality, a view of time
somewhat similar to that of Saint Augustine.

The other aspect of *Animal of Depth* exemplified in this poem is
that of the lexical innovations. In the first stanza the adjective
lucidera appears, a coined word which the poet prefers—probably
because it is more euphonious—to a half dozen others, of similar
meaning, accepted by the Spanish Academy. In the second stanza
the poet introduces a new verb, *soñear,* also without the sanction of
the academy, a fact which in itself may have enhanced its appeal to
him. It may also have been his intention to emphasize one meaning
of *soñar,* already used in the stanza, to the exclusion of others, not
simply *dream* but *daydream.* The variant may have been suggested
by some verb ending in *-ear,* such as *fantasear.* Two new nouns
occur at the end of the stanza, *ultratierra* ("ultraland") and
ultracielo ("ultrasky"), both derived from *ultramar* ("ultrasea")
just as *pleacielo* and *pleadios* had been suggested by *pleamar* in an
earlier poem, and combinations of adjectives and nouns, or of two
nouns, had produced such neologisms as *verdemar* ("greensea"),

amarillomar ("yellowsea"), *ríomar* ("riversea"), *niñodios* ("childgod"). In the fourth stanza Jiménez invents the verbal *plenitente* ("plenitent") used as an adjective modifying *conciencia*.

The coined words used in *Animal of Depth* would make an extensive list. The device is considered by some critics to have contributed to the enrichment of Jiménez' poetic language and to its heightened precision.[67] However, the opposite point of view is equally defensible. "With My Half There" is repetitious, diffuse, somewhat nebulous and sentimental, but this poem is not the most typical of the collection. Some critics regard *Animal of Depth* as the summit of Jiménez' creative achievement.[68] In it an old poet had set an example of renewed faith and enthusiasm for a disenchanted generation. *Animal of Depth* was a welcome antidote for the despair that had poisoned much of contemporary literature. In this work the poet's introversion had not excluded an awareness of universal human aspirations. His "mysticism" had not transported him to a state inaccessible to men of flesh, blood, and spirit. On the contrary, he had identified himself with them, perhaps more completely than in any previous work.

VI   Desired and Desiring God

Although the sequel to *Animal of Depth*, the second part of *Desired and Desiring God*, was left incomplete, it has been possible to "complete" it posthumously, approximating what must have been Jiménez' intention the finished work should be.[69] To the seven published poems[70] were added twenty-one others, most of them left in manuscript form, all of them similar in theme and style. There is little that differentiates the majority of these poems from those of *Animal of Depth*. Some were composed on board the same ship, and in these the buoyant tone persists. However, once Jiménez' happy journey was over and it began to recede in time, he was again beset by doubt and anxiety. These sentiments pervade the poem *"Tu, secreto filón, rosadiamante"* ("You, Secret Vein, Rosediamond"). Here the poet momentarily loses contact with his god: "Suddenly, now do you shut me out / again? Are you preparing a winter for me / without you, sun of this mean life?" (*¿De pronto, ahora te me cierras / otra vez? ¿Un invierno me* *preparas / sin ti, sol de esta baja vida?"*).[71] It is significant that the poem does not end on this note. The poet conquers his despair, convincing himself that his god is only sleeping. Evoking the god of beauty, with whom he had communed in the past, his faith is restored. This is the god whose beauty was manifested in the rose, who was symbolized by the rose, and whom he now calls "rosegod". The poem ends with a curious merging of symbols, the rose and the diamond becoming the "rosediamond" (*rosadiamante*) of the "mine", of the "secret vein", the metaphors now used to identify the center of the poet's being where his god is present in secret.

In "La Tierra de los terrenales" ("The Earth of the Earth Dwellers") the poet addresses his god in praise of the earthly beings with body and soul who share the natural world with him, and who are in loving communication with him. Perhaps no other poem Jiménez wrote expresses so explicitly his love of humanity, his benign acceptance of his earthly destiny and his untroubled anticipation of death. In the final stanza the poet, in tune with life and death and with nature, meditates with serenity on the end of his earthly existence, expressing himself with simplicity and beauty:

> This is the intimate prelude
> of what is to be, to be of me
> (what now I leave behind; with the burning
> of my fervent aspiration) in the ember,
> (like the dry leaf released in smoke
> in memory and ash)
> which in her bosom soon
> the earth of the earth dwellers will gradually extinguish,
> she who will envelop both of us
> with her tenderness and with her sympathy.

> Este es el íntimo preludio
> de la entrada del resto, de mi resto
> (lo que voy dejando; con mi quema
> de ilusión fervorosa) en el rescoldo,
> (como la hoja seca separada en humo,
> en recuerdo y ceniza)
> que luego irá apagando en su regazo
> la tierra de los terrenales,
> que nos rodeará a los dos

con su ternura y con su simpatía.

(DD, 205)

In "El desnudo infinito" ("The Naked Infinite"), the first of the three final poems of *Desired and Desiring God,* the sentiment of conformity and contentment with the present world is reaffirmed. This prose poem begins with the poet's entreaty to his god not to overpower him with brilliance but to leave him each day's light, sufficient for his world—"Leave me with my eyes on what is mine, leave me with my fire of the sun, carbon and light of every hour; with the light of my green grass..."—words reminiscent of Jose Marti's entreaty that he be allowed to leave the world by the "natural" door, resting on green leaves, his face turned to the sun. [72] Jiménez, who held that the miraculous was everywhere around him in the world in which he lived, asked for nothing more than the "love of each day and bread of each day and light of each day; and shadow and peace of each night..." (DD, 216).

The search for God is the emotional source of the two poems with which *Desired and Desiring God* ends. In *"Un Dios en blanco"* ("An Unlimited God") the poet seeks a direct vision of God without the ritual and paraphernalia which men have interposed between Him and His seekers, obscuring rather than disclosing His "clean light". The face that Jiménez now writes God with a capital letter is undoubtedly of some psychological significance. The poet now yearns to return to his childhood perception of God, to experience a renewal, to die and to be reborn as the "childgod" he once was in Moguer in Spain. The poem has the ring of sincerity, and in its religious sentiment there is less ambiguity than in most of the poems of *Animal of Depth.* In his early years, as some of his poems attest, he had been a believer. Now he aspires to recapture his childhood faith, as if mindful of the words of Christ, "Whosoever shall not receive the kingdom of God as a little child, he shall not enter therein". [73]

The concluding poem of *Desired and Desiring God,* perhaps more than any other in the collection, points to the spiritual kinship between Jiménez and his two countrymen, Miguel de Unamuno and Antonio Machado, who, like him, were seekers of God. The poem is at once an earnest questioning and a prayer, direct, simple and moving.

Whether Infinite Beauty Answers ME or Not

Seeking you as I am seeking you
I cannot offend you, God,[74] whoever you are,
nor can you be a being of offense.

If I can, and I know that I can, hear
you in all the mystery which you are,
and you do not tell me I am (offending you) as I ask you,
I am not offending you.

And I know I think of you
with my most loving thoughts
in the truth of beauty,
the beauty of truth which is my calling.
And, if I think of you thus,
I cannot offend you.

Thanks I always give you. To whom do I give them?
To infinite beauty, I give them,
which I am quite capable of attaining;
which you have touched, which is you.

Whether infinite beauty answers me or not,
I know that I do not offend you, nor do I offend her.

Si la belleza inmensa me responde o no

Buscándote como te estoy buscando
yo no puedo ofenderte, Dios, el que tú seas;
ni tu podrías ser ente de ofensa.

Si yo te puedo, y yo lo sé que yo te puedo, oír
todo el misterio que tú eres,
y tú me lo dices como te lo pregunto,
yo no estoy ofendiéndote.

Y yo sé que te pienso
de la mejor manera que yo quiero,
en verdad de belleza,
belleza de verdad que es mi carrera.
Y, si te pienso así

yo no puedo ofenderte.

Gracias, yo te las doy siempre. ¿A quién las doy?
A la belleza inmensa, se las doy,
que yo soy bien capaz de conseguir;
que tú has tocado, que eres tú.

Si la belleza inmensa me responde o no,
yo sé que no te ofendo ni la ofendo.

(DD, 225-226)

In this poem there is none of the atmosphere of confidence and enthusiasm typical of those of *Animal of Depth*. *Desired and Desiring God* ends on a much more sober note than do any of those poems. Now the poet is haunted by an anxiety that is never assuaged; his posture is a more humble one than in any of the poems of *Animal of Depth*. Yet his very doubt confirms his sincerity. It is of this sort of anguish that Emily Dickinson wrote, "I like a look of agony / because I know it's true". If doubts were equated to denial, the names of many saints would probably have to be stricken from the calendar. The concluding poem of *Desired God* is a more convincing demonstration of religious faith than almost any of Jiménez' earlier poems precisely because of the poet's "look of agony" as he seeks God.

In "Camino de fe" ("Road of Faith"), an unpublished manuscript evidently intended to be a prologue to *Desired God* when that work was completed and published, Jiménez gave what was probably the most explicit statement he ever made of his religious views.[75] Although even here there are contradictions, he clearly shows his emotional identity with Christianity, not only in his childhood but also in his manhood:

As a man I began to read what Jesus the Nazarene, the Jesus of Mary, left in word, not in writing, and his clear, simple, clean and generous word, good in short, made me love him, this is the word, and I had faith in his word which also spoke of Paradise; and that Paradise, the Paradise of Jesus of Nazareth, I conceived it to be beautiful, very beautiful. When I read for the first time what Jesus crucified said to the good robber, "Today shalt thou be with me in Paradise", I was with them, and for the first time, in Paradise.[76]

Both beauty and truth are inherent in Jiménez' concept of Jesus. God is love. Beauty is Paradise, in which the poet will survive; Christ and the Father are there, if we understand them through their word and through the written testimony about them. Briefly summarized, these are his convictions. There is little in them that the orthodox Catholic would find worthy of censure, but he might be outraged by Jiménez' arbitrary dismissal of the church as an unnecessary intermediary between him and Christ:

...I go to His unadorned word without any futile scholastic commentary, without saintly priests, without Popes, without walls, I go to His word isolated from The Book as to a field of daisies in the human spring or to a mirror of light in the human winter. [77]

About three years before his death Jiménez was confined in a Puerto Rican hospital recuperating from one of his chronic depressions. Since the hospital belonged to a religious order, the poet was attended by sisters of the order, just as he had been earlier in similar circumstances. Often he dramatized his illness by repeating in lugubrious tones "Today I am going to die; today I am going to die". One day one of the sisters passing by the poet's door was greatly alarmed by what she heard. Unaware that the patient was in much less serious condition than his words had given her to believe, she rushed in to assure him that she would bring a confessor at once. Jiménez reared up in consternation, ready to bolt from his bed in order to avoid a confrontation with a confessor. None was necessary, he told the nun with some vehemence. "I am on very good terms with God". [78]

Toward the end of his life, after the death of Zenobia, there is evidence that there was a reconciliation between Jiménez and the church. The poet's nephew and heir, Francisco Hernández Pinzón y Jiménez, states that Jiménez was grieved that he had not been called to Zenobia's bedside when the last sacraments were administered to her. Later the nephew proposed that Jiménez himself receive the last sacraments, a suggestion which seemed to please the poet, and which he accepted. Hernández Pinzón then brought a priest who performed the last rites of the church, and as Osvaldo Lira puts it, "Juan Ramón died thus in the bosom of the Catholic Church". [79]

Since Jiménez' return to the church was an eleventh hour

"conversion", even his latest poems could not reflect any change in his spiritual or esthetic orientation. However, it is unlikely that there would have been any marked changes in any poems written after he had made his peace with the church. The compilation of his *Tercera antologia poética* (*Third Poetic Anthology*) occupied much of his time toward the end of his life.[80] The book, his last, came off the press in April 1957. It contains poems written as early as 1898 and as late as 1953, a large part of those published in his earlier anthologies. The complete collection of *Ballads of Coral Gables,* the three complete parts of *Space*, all of the poems of *Animal of Depth* and seven poems of *Desired and Desiring God* are also included.

Nearly all of the individual poems published in magazines during the last ten years of Jiménez' life reappear in the *Third Anthology.*[81] The volume ends, appropriately, with a poem unquestionably addressed to Zenobia, although her name is not mentioned in it. The dates (1951-1953) under the title of the group of poems with which the anthology ends would indicate that the last poem was written at the time Zenobia was being treated for the cancer which eventually took her life. In its sonnet form and its imagery it is a reversion to an earlier manner, but it is a moving tribute to the poet's wife. As the sun sets, its golden light fades on the leaves of a tree and reddens in the sky. The gold becomes shadow, "your color", says the poet, expressing his presentiment of the death of the one to whom he is speaking. In spite of its conventionality of form and theme, the poem has the beauty of emotional depth and sincerity which entitle it to the place it occupies in the anthology.

CHAPTER 6

Prose Works

I Platero and I

ONCE critics and the reading public have conveniently classified an author as novelist, dramatist, essayist or poet, he is not likely to gain easy recognition for writings not identifiable by the accepted label. Jiménez sometimes complained that many of his readers were unaware that he wrote prose as well as poetry. He had written articles, sketches, vignettes and caricatures throughout his leterary career but only one prose work, *Platero y yo* (*Platero and I*), a notable exception, won widespread literary acclaim. Jiménez himself was, perhaps, more to blame for this public indifference or ignorance than anyone else. While published volumes of his poetry followed one another in close succession from 1900 to 1923, his prose pieces were not collected and printed in volumes but remained dispersed throughout the magazines, newspapers and notebooks in which they originally appeared. Not until after his death were most of them made accessible to the general public.[1]

The first edition of *Platero and I* was published in 1914; the definitive edition, considerably longer than the first, appeared in 1917, both printed in Madrid. The popularity of *Platero* has been enormous, not only in the Spanish-speaking countries—where it is required reading in schools—but throughout the Western world. The many translations into other languages [2] attest the universality of its appeal.

Platero is a collection of prose poems, sketches or vignettes—it is difficult to find a word that identifies them accurately—each of which may be read independently, but which taken together form a unified work. There is no narrative continuity. The unity of *Platero* is achieved in part through the setting—Moguer and its environs—recreated in the sketches with remarkable concision and sensitivity. They are never marred by prolixity or abuse of local color. Their unity is enhanced more by selectivity than by

122

profuseness of detail. Jiménez had a keen eye for the significant features of physical reality and a faculty for translating them, with maximum verbal economy, into clean-cut imagery. Thus there emerges from the sparely drawn poetic sketches the vision of a town and a milieu which have life, character and authenticity, more authenticity than one might expect of an author whose earlier works had often been tinged with excessive sentimentality. *Platero* reveals with subtlety both the charm and the sordidness of Moguer and its society. It is in some ways comparable to Sherwood Andersons *Winesburg, Ohio,* a book which Jiménez admired and of which he often spoke.[3] Both works recreate the life of a whole town with an insight and profundity which their simple, lucid prose might seem to belie. In *Platero,* to a greater extent than in *Winesburg, Ohio*, the lyric, not the narrative or descriptive aspect of the work is its distinguishing feature.

The unity of *Platero* is further sustained by the two "characters", the author himself and his donkey, Platero, who appear together in nearly all of the prose poems. It can be argued that Platero is in reality only a literary device that enables Jiménez to carry on what one critic calls a "Lyric monologue" ("monólogo lírico").[4] Of course, Platero and his master do not carry on a conversation in the conventional sense, but there is communication between them. Platero has ways of showing that he understands what his master says. The humanization of the donkey is one of the most appealing features of Platero.[5] An affectionate relationship exists between the poet and the beast on which he rides through town and countryside. Platero is delineated with whimsy, humor, tenderness and sympathy. In his prose poems Jiménez is reliving his own experiences. *Platero and I* is actually a lyric autobiography. The little donkey, presented sympathetically in the book, is not wholly a literary creation but had a living counterpart whose master was the poet.[6]

There is, of course, no lack of antecedents in Spanish cultural tradition for the appearance of four-footed characters in literature—Rocinante and Babieca to cite two famous examples—quite apart from their use in fables. The tradition continues in *Platero and I*. Without Platero, Jiménez might have written a series of short prose pieces of high artistic merit on his native town, but such a work would have lacked the warmth and the intimate character which Platero gives to the one which bears his name.

There is throughout the book an attitude of Franciscan tenderness toward animals in general, which is often strongly reminiscent of Francis Jammes, another of Jiménez' favorite authors. Jammes devotes almost as much attention in his stories and poems to the fauna, both wild and domestic, of his native Basque country of France as to the human characters in them. The same is true of Jiménez in *Platero and I.* Donkeys, horses, bulls, dogs, chickens, ducks, sparrows, a parrot, a canary, a turtle, butterflies and other creatures all live, move and have their being in the world of *Platero.* Both Jammes and Jiménez considered animals, donkeys in particular, as worthy of a happier afterlife in paradise, after their earthly afflictions had ended. [7]

After Platero's death the poet visits his grave and speaks to him, much as he did when the little donkey was still alive: "Platero my friend...if you are now in a field in heaven as I think you are, carrying youthful angels on your soft furry back, I wonder if perhaps you have forgotten me. Tell me, Platero, do you still remember me?"[8] Jiménez dedicates his volume of prose poems to "Platero in the Heaven of Moguer". One of the selections he entitled "Asnografía" ("Donkeyography"), a defense of the donkey, humorous and ironic toward men, but in its love and compassion for the animal it is similar to a eulogy of the donkey in one of Jammes' stories.[9] "Donkeyography" begins thus:

I read in a dictionary: "Donkeyography: N. Used ironically to describe the donkey".

Poor donkey! Good, noble, quick-witted as you are! Ironically,—why? Do you not even deserve a serious description, you whose true description would be a story of springtime? Why, they should call the man who is good, Donkey! And the donkey who is bad, Man. Ironically—to say this of you, so intellectual, such a friend to old and young, to stream and butterfly, to sun and dog, flower and moon; so patient and thoughtful, melancholy and loveable, the Marcus Aurelius of the meadows.[10]

The realism with which Jiménez recreates the life of Moguer is achieved with a minimum of descriptive detail, but it is unusually effective in bringing the town and countryside to life, with their quaintness and beauty, their harshness and inhumanity. The secret seems to lie in Jiménez' ability to discover or sense what is beneath the surface of what he observes. The reality of this Moguer is more empathic than photographic. It is a reality of living beings.

Whether humans or animals, what they most commonly inspire is pathos. "El potro castrado" ("The Gelding"), undoubtedly based on a first-hand knowledge of farm life, is the reaction of a sensitive person to the unreasoned brutality with which a handsome young stallion is shorn of the splendor of its virility and spirit. "El perro sarnoso" ("The Mangy Dog") is an expression of pity for a homeless dog, stoned by humans, snarled at by other dogs and finally killed by a shotgun blast fired by an unthinking watchman. "El canario se muere" ("The Canary Dies") is an elegy in memory of a canary so old that in the last months of its life it could no longer sing. The poet confides to Platero: "Listen: tonight, the children, you and I will take the dead bird down to the garden. The moon is full now and beneath its pallid silver, the poor singer will look, in the white hand of Blanca, like a withered petal from a golden iris. And we shall bury him under the large rose bush."[11]

Two other sketches, "La yegua blanca" ("The White Mare") and "El burro viejo" ("The Old Donkey"), are similar to those mentioned above. Both express a compassionate concern for suffering animals, particularly those afflicted with old age and physical decrepitude, but they are, as well, an implicit commentary on the universal human condition.

Jiménez, never a respecter of wealth, authority and social prestige, paid scant attention to the elite of Moguer, the class to which he actually belonged. There is virtually no mention of the town's "influential" citizens except in the context of irony. "Don José, the Village Priest", is an example of this treatment. The sight of the priest moves the poet to make the following remarks to Platero:

Now, Platero, he is riding along sanctimoniously and speaking honeyed words. But the one who in fact is always angelic is his she-donkey, a real lady.

I believe that you saw him one day in his orchard, wearing sailor's trousers and a broad-brimmed hat, hurling insults and stones at the little boys who were stealing his oranges....

Never have I heard a man use worse language, nor call to higher heaven with his oaths. It is true, that he knows, or so he says in his five o'clock mass, where heaven is and how everything is arranged there. Trees, earth, water, wind, flame: all these, so full of grace, so soft, so fresh, so pure, so alive, seem to serve him only as examples of disorder, hardness, coldness, violence and destruction. At the end of each day every stone in his orchard comes to rest in a different spot, after being thrown in furious hostility at birds, and washerwomen, children and flowers. [12]

Frasco Vélez, the mayor of Moguer, does not appear in person in the sketch which bears his name, but it does contain the text of an absurd ordinance he has posted in the town square. The ordinance announces in pompous terms that all dogs not on a leash will be summarily shot. The mayor has his minions—whom he grandly designates as the "municipal guards"—roaming the town and surrounding areas shooting "rabid dogs". It is rumored about town that the shooting keeps the townspeople inside their homes, leaving the mayor free to dispose of his contraband agave and fig brandy.

In contrast to the disparaging view of these town dignitaries there is in *Platero and I* a consistent attitude of sympathy toward the humble, the poor, the unfortunate. It is the first time, as some critics have noted, that the poet has emerged from his somewhat fatuous egocentricity and has manifested a concern for the humanity around him.[13] A half-witted boy; the little daughter of a charcoal vendor, "pretty and dirty as a coin"; a friendless and despised Puerto Rican servant; a ragged little girl and an emaciated donkey trying vainly to extricate their cart from the muddy stream bed in which it is stuck; gypsies; poor children; men and women afflicted by age, sorrow, neglect—all these are objects of Jiménez' attention and are treated with understanding and sympathy. The emotion is spontaneous and never serves as a pretext for interpolating a social message, a political harangue or a sermon. A glimpse of an individual or a situation is sufficient for Jiménez to discover its essential reality. The emotional repercussions of the discovery, translated into simple, succinct and sensitive language, often give the prose poems a surprising impact on the reader's sensibility. He is capable not only of vivid visualization of a scene or incident but also of emotional identification with the human participants.[14]

In "Games at Dusk" a number of poor children are playing in a dry riverbed at nightfall. As the poet and Platero approach, they are pretending to be beggars, one feigning blindness, another lameness, others joining in the play in different ways. Jiménez continues:

Then comes one of those sudden changes that happen with children; since they are wearing shoes and clothes, and their mothers, in some way known only to them, have given them food to eat, they think themselves princes.

"My father has a silver watch."

"And mine has a horse."

"And mine a shotgun."

A watch that will get him up at dawn, a gun that—will not kill hunger, a horse that will lead to poverty.

Then they form a circle. Amid so much blackness, a little girl with a thin voice—a thread of liquid crystal in the dark—sings melodiously as a princess:

"I'm the young widow of the Count of Oré. ..."[15]

Until he was nearly twenty Jiménez had lived entirely in Andalusia, a region always popular with writers, painters and travelers in quest of local color. He never disclaimed his provincial antecedents nor tried to conceal them. Throughout his career he acknowledged their importance in his formation and their sentimental hold in his life. Yet regionalism for its own sake had little esthetic and human significance to him. He had no objection to being called "The Universal Andalusian" ("El andaluz universal") as he sometimes was, quite appropriately. Andalusia, typified by Moguer, lives in *Platero and I,* but within a more transcendent perspective than is generally found in *costumbrista* sketches and regional novels. The color and pageantry of local festivals are not wholly excluded from *Platero* but their treatment is one of understatement. Jiménez had no fondness for public gaiety, unless it was the spontaneous gaiety of children in their natural circumstances. By them he was fascinated and toward them he was always amiable, generous and responsive. Among the most charming sketches in *Platero* are those which apprehend the anxiety and the joy of children, the play of their fantasy, their instinctive perception of the beauty of the world around them.

In all the Spanish-speaking countries, Carnival is celebrated with display and revelry. An episode in *Platero* which bears the title "Carnival" describes the celebration and the participation of the poet and his donkey in it. Platero, decked out in gay trappings, is caught up in a maelstrom of shouting, laughing and dancing humanity. Nervous and bewildered, he tries to escape, but he is trapped in a circle of wildly singing and dancing citizens, amid a din of brass instruments, tambourines, clanging, braying and laughter. In desperation he finally plunges through the revelers and runs to his master. "Like me"—says the poet—"he wants nothing to do with Carnival. We were not made for this sort of thing".[16] Both his temperament and his esthetic convictions gave Jiménez a distaste for things showy and superficial and for gregarious cavorting. To him the raucous merrymaking, the glitter and the "local color" of popular festivals seemed a distortion of the real Moguer.

The "Bull Fight" is not, as one might expect, a description of the spectacle which throughout the world passes for something typically Spanish. One sentiment it does express is the poet's aversion to bull fights. While the town is agog with excitement over the approaching event, he and Platero leave by a back lane for the country, just as they had the previous year:

How beautiful the countryside is these festival days when everyone abandons it. In the vineyards and vegetable gardens one sees scarcely a single old man bending over the brittle vine or the pure stream. In the distance there rises over the town, like a jester's crown, the full clamor of the crowd, the clapping, and the music from the bull ring, all of which we lose as we go serenely towards the sea. And the soul, Platero, feels truly queen of all it surveys by virtue of its own feelings and of the great sound body of Nature, who when respected gives to those who are worthy the spectacle of her splendid and eternal beauty. [17]

In spite of the intrusion of a somewhat atypical didactic note, the passage expresses something fundamental in Jiménez' esthetics and his conception of the world. Unlike Baudelaire, with whom there is, nevertheless, a link through the Symbolists,[18] he saw nature as a benevolent force and an inexhaustible source of beauty. Throughout *Platero*, just as in his other works, the attitude persists. The most characteristic feature of this work is its lyricism,[19] most often a direct response to sights, colors, sounds, scents and forms in the natural world. The following passage, rich in aural imagery, is an exultant song of praise to the Creator and His creation:

I go out to the orchard and thank God for the blue day. Unrestrained concert from fresh throats without number! Capriciously, the swallow sends her warbling spiraling down the well; the blackbird whistles over the fallen orange; the fire-bright oriole chatters in the oak; the titmouse spins long, fine laughter from the top of the eucalyptus; and in the great pine, the sparrows carry on a turbulent discussion.

What a morning it is! The sun scatters over the earth its gold and silver joy; butterflies of a hundred hues play everywhere, among the flowers, through the house, in the fountain. The fields all around burst and crack open in a ferment of healthy new life.

We seem to be within a great honeycomb of light, the burning center of an immense flaming rose. [20]

This passage, like many similar ones, demonstrates that the poetic quality of *Platero* is partly achieved by the use of an elliptical prose almost as rigorous in its demands as poetry of fixed form. There is little room for verbiage in a sonnet, and in *Platero* there is a somewhat similar restraint, or reduction to the essential. Synecdoche is used twice at the beginning of the paragraph: "blue day", "throats without number". No verb precedes the latter, nor is any needed. The auditory imagery is particularly effective. The song and the habits of each bird are identified with poetic precision: the swallow's "warblings spiraling down the well", the titmouse in the eucalyptus spinning "long, fine, laughter", the "turbulent discussion" of the sparrows in the pine tree. The metaphors combine freshness, fantasy and verisimilitude.

In each prose poem, there is commonly a mere thread of exposition, a descriptive element reduced to a nucleus of reality, the bare hint of its totality, then the subjective vibrations activated by it, expressed an imagery elaborated with subtlety, sensitivity and beauty. *Platero* anticipates the elevation of the common, the humble, the quotidian to poetic dignity, an innovation which subsequently came into general use among Hispanic poets. Jiménez was among the first to reject the dramatic, the spectacular, the elegant and the exotic as essential or desirable in poetic creation. In *Platero* the simplest act of daily routine is often the prelude to a poetic experience. Innumerable examples like the following could be quoted:

Platero had just drunk two pails of starlight water from the well in the corral and was returning to the stable, slowly and absent-mindedly between the tall sunflowers....

Beyond the low roof, damp from the September mildness, the far fields lay sleeping, giving off a strong scent of pine. A great black cloud, like a gigantic hen laying a golden egg, left the moon upon the hill.[21]

Critics have, with some frequency, spoken of the impressionistic imagery in Jiménez' poetry but they have had little to say about this aspect of his prose.[22] However, throughout *Platero* the poet exhibits a painter's alertness and sensitivity to light, color and form and their subtle mutations through the hours of the day. The following two examples are typical:

When I go to see Platero at noon, a clear ray from the midday sun lights up a great patch of gold on the soft silver of his back. Beneath his belly, on the dark floor of uncertain green, the old roof rains down clear coins of fire.[23]

. . . .

Over the still-flowering roses the afternoon slowly declines. The glow of the sunset catches the last roses and the whole garden, rising like a flame of fragrance toward the blaze of the setting sun, smells of burned roses. Silence.[24]

In *Platero* visual imagery is, without doubt, more often employed than any other, but this prose is in general rich in sensory content. Sometimes a short passage, like the following, all but runs the gamut of sensory impressions, not only visual, but auditory, gustatory, and tactile as well: "...When we reach the shade of the large walnut tree, I split two watermelons, which open their scarlet-and-rose frost work with a long, cool-sounding creak. I eat mine slowly, listening to the faraway ringing of vespers in the town. Platero drinks up the sugary flesh of his as if it were water".[25]

Platero and I appeared opportunely at a time when many men viewed with growing apprehension the encroachment of industrialism and mechanization on the environment in which they lived. The exodus from rural to urban areas was under way; men were being absorbed by the cities with their clangor, confusion, sordidness and loneliness in rapidly increasing numbers. *Platero and I* is a reassuring vision of an environment in which man is not

yet lost in the anonymity of the masses, and in which his close
relationship to nature has not yet been subverted. The town at
nightfall is a scene of tranquility and beauty, in which life has
meaning and continuity.

An odor drifts from the clean full grain which stands in vague yellowish
mounds on the threshing floors, under the cool stars. The workers sing
softly in dreamy weariness. Seated in the doorways, the widows think of
the dead who are sleeping so near, behind the corrals. The children run
from one shadow to another as birds go from tree to tree. [26]

Platero and I is the preservation in art of a world epitomized by
Moguer and its countryside. What sustains the harmony of
existence in this environment is the integration of life in the village
with that of the surrounding rural area. Man is not separated from
other men, nor from nature. The town dweller and the rustic are
alike in their consciousness of their dependence on nature, in their
awe or apprehension in its presence, in their response—much as it
varies among them—to nature, to which they themselves belong.
To a greater extent than in any other of his works Jiménez identifies himself with the humanity around him. On the esthetic plane,
Platero and I achieves with simple language a poetic quality that is
notable for the sheer beauty and the suggestiveness of its imagery.
The following is an example, of the many that could be selected
almost at random:

A large moon comes with us, round and pure. Vaguely, in the drowsy
meadows one can see strange black goats among the brambles. Someone
hides silently as we pass.... Above the fence an immense almond tree,
snowy with blossoms and moonlight, its tops mingled with a white cloud,
shelters the path from arrows shot by March stars.... A pungent scent of
oranges.... Dampness, silence.... [27]

In its universality, *Platero and I* is perhaps unsurpassed by any of
Jiménez' other works. The poet himself took care to correct the
mistaken assumption that it was written for children, asserting: "I
have never written anything for children, because I believe that the
child can read what the man reads, with certain exceptions that
come to everyone's mind...." [28] Several generations of readers in
many lands have demonstrated the accessibility of *Platero and I* to
young and old alike, and their appreciation both of its human and
its esthetic values.

II   Españoles de tres mundos (Spaniards of Three Worlds)[29]

Jiménez once stated that *Platero and I* was the most representative prose work of his "first period" and *Spaniards of Three Worlds* the most representative of the second.[30] What he probably meant was not that the latter was the most typical, but the one that in his judgment was his most original work. Certainly it is the most unusual, something quite different from the most representative.

Spaniards of Three Worlds is made up of sixty-one short "lyric caricatures", as the author called them, some of his living contemporaries, others of persons no longer living.[31] In the prologue Jiménez admits his intentional use of a baroque style in many of the caricatures, a genre which, he asserted, Quevedo had found well-suited to baroque treatment. The subject of the caricature is most often a man of letters, sometimes a statesman, a painter or a musician. The portrayal is both physical and psychological; the antecedents and the environment of the individual are usually accessory to the interpretation of the personality and the work.[32]

As one might expect there is a lyric portrait of Gustavo Adolfo Bécquer, the poet to whom Jiménez probably owed more than to any other of his countrymen. Bécquer's lyric caricature, the first in *Spaniards of Three World,* is in many ways representative of the collection as a whole. It is translated in its entirety.

Gustavo Adolfo Bécquer

(1870)

Bécquer extends a hand, casts himself into the round gale and with it emerges from the large honeysuckle, his momentary refuge from the sudden thunder shower of May, a pleasing instant of soft fragrant shadow for his desperation. Trembling, cyanotic, coughing, clutching at the same time his restless top hat against the high wave, he wraps, a difficult struggle, in the short cape which scarcely shelters him from the chill of the minute of the between-season green and cyclone, dust and drop, the unreal harp. Did he seize it, then, that morning in the dark corner of the salon, its naked strings full, like the almond in bloom, with sleeping wings? Where is he taking it to open its notes? What confusion: honeysuckle, choking, unseasonableness, woman, chill, ideal, harp! Harp or woman, string or arm, dream; all intangible love:

(Sealing with a kiss her treason).

He has, piercing the center of the plaza of the soul, an echo, and it keeps hurting him like the enlarged thorn of an orange tree, an unbearable angina of the chest, which perhaps does not kill the first time. To moderate such persistent pain and see if he can be rid of it through the river of his blood, his heart, a veiled drum, beats out even more its second aortic tone, which gives his total hearing, from heel to temple, under the black cloud of asphyxiation, that sharp, muted assonance of his, reinforcement of the second poetic tone, plumb of a dark hypertrophied heart. Anxiety fallen in definitive "discompensation" against the white, mauve and gold flights of fantasy. And with that cordial assonance, he changes, makes his, he eternizes, because it is life, it is accent, the Spanish verse of his hour:

(Today the sun reaches the depth of my soul).

Around Bécquer, like the supreme ideal flower, yellow and silver, among birds which all together crown it, their ardent chirping bills toward it. Rhyme flies, a vulgar thing in so many, before and after; unique, authentic in him, just as his hard gray assonance is singular. Assonance, Rhyme can no longer be used for many years in Spain without coming back from Bécquer. Assonance, Rhyme, Rhyme,, Assonance. Rhyme, the Rhyme of black and white breast, sheltered in the coat of arms of the portico, in the stone tomb, in the wall of the convent, in the closed balcony with the Sevillan sunset, green and rose of water and sun, in its glass. The assonance of the heart, the Rhyme swallow. (Better Romanticism, hidden, exact, restrained, in the fatal atmosphere of the time.) The short Rhyme, Bécquer, the deep Assonance. [33]

In any caricature there must be, presumably, an underlying reality, features of which the caricaturist may exaggerate or distort to suit his ends, but not to the extent that the resulting image lose all resemblance to the original. In Jiménez' best caricatures the subject is not lost in the bewildering maze of metaphors and distorted syntax which he often uses in his portrayal. Fact and fantasy are interwoven in varying proportions in what is more an intuitive than an intellectual creative process. At their best the caricatures illuminate previously undisclosed facets of a personality or a work; at their worst they lapse into grotesque nonsense.

In the trembling, wheezing, corporeal Bécquer the author accentuates the infirmity of the poet—an unhappy reality of his existence—presenting him with pathos, not with irony or humor as one usually éxpects in caricatures. The sentiment is intensified by representing Bécquer as braving a violent May storm, attempting to protect his harp from the elements by covering it with the short cape with which he can scarcely shelter himself from rain and wind. The unseasonable storm is a metaphor which most plausibly refers to the disdain and disapproval with which Bécquer's countrymen received his poetry during his lifetime, ignoring the merits which later generations discovered in his work.

The honeysuckle which had been Bécquer's momentary refuge from the storm can be identified as those moments of his troubled existence when he experienced love or had fleeting glimpses of transcendent beauty in the world about him. The "ideal harp", Bécquer's poetry, as Predmore has pointed out,[34] is a metaphor which, like "honeysuckle", conveys a suggestion of the subtle, subjective tone and quality of the Sevillan poet's verse. Perhaps Jiménez' most effective metaphor is that of the heart beat which gives Bécquer the rhythmic pattern for his verse. The accented assonance peculiar to Bécquer is thus the spontaneous metrical expression of his profound inner anguish. It is the very beating of his afflicted heart. No one has paid higher tribute than Jiménez to Bécquer's instinctive skill at adapting the form of his poetry to its emotional content.

The caricature of Bécquer illustrates as well as any other the merits and limitations of a style which with less frequency attains the sublime than the grotesque. In the baroque manner he consciously cultivated, Jiménez relied mainly on tortuous syntax and prodigality of imagery. The sentence is often a long succession of parenthetical clauses, interspersed with series of adjectival and adverbial elements, disparate and startling images. In this forest it is sometimes difficult to distinguish the trees.[35] The caricature of Bécquer is achieved with originality and insight, but it is also repetitive, redundant, ornate, rhetorically complex, as if Jiménez had deliberately set himself the task of writing in a manner he normally shunned. The final paragraph of "Gustavo Adolfo Bécquer", to cite one example, is an accumulation of heterogeneous images in which the concrete and the abstract, forms, sounds and colors are scrambled indiscriminately, similar to the confusion to which Jiménez himself refers at the end of his opening paragraph.

The designation "lyric caricature" is in itself paradoxical. The genre may have been better suited to satire than lyric treatment, something which may be adduced from some of the sketches themselves. Mordant satire was a weapon Jiménez wielded with dexterity. In some of the caricatures he shows a closer kinship to Quevedo than to Bécquer. One of the longest and most corrosive sketches is that of Pablo Neruda, whom he characterizes in the opening sentence as "a great poet, a great bad poet". The metaphors Jiménez uses here are numerous but not nebulous as in some of the other sketches, since incisiveness and nebulosity are, in effect, mutually exclusive.

> (Neruda) possesses a depository of everything he has come across in his world, a sort of dumping ground, at times a manure pile, where there has turned up among the discards, the waste, the debris, some stone, or flower, a piece of metal still in good condition, still beautiful. He finds the rose, the diamond, the gold, but not the representative and transforming word; he does not replace the subject or the object with his word; he transfers object and subject, not substance nor essence.... [36]

Perhaps no book Jiménez ever wrote has been more enthusiastically praised or more caustically criticized than *Spaniards of Three Worlds*. Ricardo Gullón, commenting on Jiménez' prose in general, finds it "as important, attractive and perfect as his verse", and ventures to ask whether *Spaniards of Three Worlds* is not one of the best prose works of this century in the Spanish language.[37] The French critic Jean-Louis Schonberg credits Jiménez with flashes of keen critical insight but finds him vituperative and unfair in many of his judgments. What is even worse, in Schonberg's opinion, is the style of Jiménez' lyric caricatures, which incorporate all the worst features of the baroque in its most exaggerated form, extravagance and incoherence.[38]

It would be difficult to accept either judgment as definitive. The caricatures may be viewed as literary experiments which are more interesting for their rhetorical innovations and their acute subjective evaluations than for their profundity, their equitableness or their art. It is doubtful that they add or detract anything from Jiménez' work judged in its totality.[39] Had another of Spain's contemporary men of letters ventured to write a book comparable to *Spaniards of Three Worlds* in its stylistic contortions, it is quite probable that Jiménez would have subjected him to a critical excoriation he would never have forgotten.

III *Literary Criticism*

In his prose, as in his poetry, Jiménez was not given to prolixity. Most of his writings are brief and somewhat fragmentary—impressions, thoughts, reminiscences of a personal character. He was fond of aphorisms and wrote many of them. The essay was not his preferred mode of expression but he published some substantial articles, most of which he first delivered as lectures. These were sometimes repeated, as the poet had occasion to address new audiences in Spain, Spanish America or the United States. His lectures and essays commonly deal with literature and particularly with his favorite genre, poetry.[40]

As a critic Jiménez was no respecter of academic literary criteria. His criticism was much more notable for its incisiveness than for its objectivity. Ricardo Gullón considers Jiménez one of the keenest literary critics of modern times, an opinion which might surprise the many who know Jiménez almost exclusively as a lyric poet. However, Gullón is careful to make one reservation in his estimate of Jiménez as a critic. He lauds the lucidity and penetration of Jiménez' critical vision when it is not obscured by some emotional bias.[41] Passionately embroiled, as the poet often was, in Spain's literary polemics of the 1920s and 1930s, the circumstances were hardly propitious for him to exercise his critical function with serenity and impartiality. "Pure and implacable", Alfonso Reyes said of him, for Jiménez' position was one of intransigence with whatever he considered mediocre, slovenly, affected or insincere, in literature and in life. His esthetic integrity demanded of him that he call these deadly sins to the attention of the reading public and the community of writers, but there seems often to have been a Mephistophelean impulse behind the dagger thrusts of irony with which he prodded and deflated his adversaries.

Jiménez, like Verlaine and Unamuno, made a distinction between poetry and literature. The former he identified as "the expression of the ineffable".[42] He further defined it as "dynamic ecstasy, the rhythmic intoxicating enchantment, the unutterable palpitating miracle from which the essential accent issues...."[43] He coincided with Poe in the contention that great poetry is nearly always brief and that narrative, didactic, descriptive and anecdotal elements did not belong in poetry. These, Jiménez would have designated as "literature", a term with a suggestion of disparagement, as he used it. He conceded that literature might attain relative beauty but poetry aspires to the attainment of absolute beauty.[44] Poetic creation was more intuitive than intellectual; by profundity in poetry Jiménez understood emotional depth not conceptual brilliance. The parrot and the peacock, he said, properly belong to the heraldry of literature, but the spirit of the poet is a lonely nightingale free of the emblazoned cage. Literature is a state of culture, poetry is a state of grace preceding and succeeding culture.[45]

The proximity of the poetic experience to the religious experience is clearly implied in Jiménez' reference to poetry as a state of grace. However, he viewed his countrymen as essentially realistic, not religious, more dogmatic than spiritual, more Catholic than Christian. Spain is a country of "roots" rather than "wings", he said, using two metaphors which recur with some frequency in his prose as well as in his poetry. As Jiménez saw it, literature flourished in Spain usually to the neglect of poetry. The court was the center of literary activity, while the spirituality and pantheism of the mystics, whom Jiménez considered to be Spain's most authentic poets, were nurtured in the solitude of monasteries and rural communities, where the austerity of a grim and rocky landscape was mitigated by the infinitude of a transparent sky. Here the poet "created his poetry, like his prayers, for himself". However, it is apparent that the seclusion of these poets did not imply a renunciation of their secular heritage. Perhaps they had assimilated popular culture as naturally as they had, throughout their lives, eaten bread for physical sustenance. The poetry they created was not solely the expression of mystic rapture but had direct popular antecedents. Jiménez considered the unwritten poetry of the people to be one of the most important sources of Spanish lyricism.[46] He associated "people" (*pueblo*) with rural and village Spain, not with its urban centers and their "proletariat", a term that to him connoted political propaganda and exploitation.[47]

In several of his critical writings Jiménez paid tribute to San Juan de la Cruz, in his opinion the most exalted of Spain's poets of the sixteenth and seventeenth centuries and perhaps his favorite of all Spanish poets. San Juan de la Cruz had a quality which Jiménez found in few poets, an essentiality which he called "accent". It is a term that eludes exact definition, but the ingenuous, tender, lexically simple poems of San Juan de la Cruz, with their metaphysical depth, their music and intensity—all these taken together—might best exemplify Spanish poetry with "accent". In contemporary Spanish poetry, that of Jiménez is clearly the best example. Critics have often commented on the kinship between these two poets.[48]

In Jiménez' view no worthy successor to San Juan de la Cruz appeared in Spanish poetry until some two and one half centuries after the mystic's death. Poetry became rhetorical in the seventeenth century, affected in the eighteenth, vulgar in the nineteenth. Even Góngora, whose genius he recognized, and whom he in some ways resembled, Jiménez referred to as "the chief pedant of literary Spain".[49] In Bécquer—not ordinarily classified by literary historians as a mystic—Jiménez discovered a close kinship with San Juan de la Cruz, and clearly identified the Sevillan poet as a mystic.[50] The "accent" so long missing from Spanish poetry reappeared in Bécquer.

Perhaps nothing written by Jiménez is a better statement of his position as a critic of Spanish contemporary literature than his essay "Crisis del espíritu en la poesía española contemporánea" ("Crisis of the Spirit in Contemporary Spanish Poetry"). Here he credits Miguel de Unamuno and Rubén Darío with the renewal which restored the spirituality and the splendor to Spanish and Spanish-American poetry. However, Jiménez insists that both poets were indebted to Bécquer, from whom the initial impulse came, and with whom contemporary Spanish poetry in reality begins.[51] The "accent" which distinguished the poetry of Jorge Manrique, Garcilaso, San Juan de la Cruz and Fray Luis de León is, thus, first renascent in Bécquer, and following him, in Unamuno and Rubén Darío. The new direction which Hispanic poetry takes toward 1900 is identified by Jiménez as Modernism, but the term never meant the same to him that it did to most critics and scholars.[52] Unamuno often spoke disparagingly of Modernism and Modernists, including Rubén Darío.[53] Had anyone identified him as Modernist, Unamuno would probably have protested with vehemence. To him Modernism was affected, morbid and superficial—*blandenguería*—he called it—the very antithesis of what he thought poetry should be. Jiménez was not an admirer of what Unamuno excoriated, but he judged Modernism by its most exalted values, not by their perversion. The two poets were not separated by any profound esthetic or moral incompatibility, quite the contrary; the difference between them was mainly one of terminology. To one of them Modernism meant degeneration, to the other renewal.

Jiménez believed that Spanish poetry of the twentieth century was revitalized by a union of opposites, the personality and esthetic principles of Unamuno with those of Rubén Darío (see Chapter II, p. 28). Their principal successors and continuers were two Andalusian poets—Antonio Machado, and another whom Jiménez declines to name, but whose identity he unmistakably establishes, Juan Ramón Jiménez. Machado incorporates into Spanish poetic tradition what Jiménez calls Unamuno's "religious modernism" and the "profane modernism" of Rubén Darío. In his poetic orientation, Machado undoubtedly owed more to Unamuno than to Darío, while the opposite was true of Jiménez. However, the relationship between the two Andalusian poets was always one of warm friendship and mutual respect. Jiménez' critique of Machado's poetry is probably the fairest he wrote on the work of any of his contemporaries. He was particularly laudatory of Machado's early poetry, *Soledades* (1903), in which he found a mysterious enchantment that delighted him. Machado's more objective *Campos de Castilla* (1912) appealed to Jiménez less, but he praised the profundity, the breadth of vision and the fidelity with which these poems interpret the spirit of Castile and of Spain. Jiménez considered Machado "the true national poet" of Spain,[54] an opinion he gave without any of the irony or innuendo that sometimes came like a slap after a caress when he spoke of his fellow poets. What Jiménez meant by "national" in this case had no chauvinistic connotation but referred to the essentiality of Machado's "Castillian" poems.[55]

Jiménez spoke somewhat summarily of his own contribution to the Spanish poetic renaissance of this century, but without in any way disguising his recognition of its importance. He stated that because of his fondness for experimentation and change, his creative enthusiasm and his ceaseless activity as a "lover of poetry", his influence was more extensive and more visible than that of Machado. He declared himself to be repentant of the sins of commission and omission that had made him a center of con- troversy and criticism. He was his own severest critic, he said; each day his own work pleased him less,[56] a rebuttal that he often used to disarm polemicists with whom he had to deal.

What drew the most devastating critical fire from Jiménez was the trend that he observed in the generation of poets that immediately followed his own. As he saw it, the universality which had been restored to Spanish poetry by Bécquer and his lineal descendants was again being lost. World War (I) was in large part responsible for the change, which was general, not limited to Spain. Jiménez reproached his successors for disowning their heritage, not because of what it might have retained of rhetorical and traditional impediments, but because they ignored or disdained its human values. The new emphasis was on ingenuity, playful intellectualism, artificiality, technical hocus-pocus and mystification. Jiménez decried the dehumanization of art, the disappearance of "emotion and ecstasy" from poetry. Among the offenders were Jorge Guillén, Pedro Salinas, Gerardo Diego, Dámaso Alonso and others he did not name. He censured them collectively for their conformity to one pattern, a repetitiousness which gave their work the revolting perfection of "machine-made lace" or of "odious stucco friezes" produced in a mold. There was no individuality, no "accent" in this poetry, said Jiménez. He characterized the authors as "talented bricklayers" or "engineers".

There is an occasional concession to the merits of some of the poets with whom he deals—José Moreno Villa, Rafael Alberti, Federico García Lorca and a few others—but Jiménez' appraisal of contemporary Spanish poets is on the whole negative, his attitude somewhat like that of an annoyed parent scolding his children for their unruliness. The many years of his life he had devoted to poetic creation, and the recognition he had won for it, gave him a position of authority throughout the Spanish-speaking world. From this vantage point he could observe the contemporary scene and praise or censure what seemed to him to deserve it, knowing that his word carried weight. He had little enthusiasm for the effervescent vanguardism of many of the poets younger than he. Listing the new "isms" by name (Ultraism, Dadaism, Surrealism, etc.), he added a few items of his own invention, a rather typical ironic twist: "interior monologuism", "biblicism", "putrefactionism", the last of these undoubtedly meant for Neruda and the imagery of his *Residencias*. Jiménez' contention was that no "authentic, natural poet" needéd or accepted the faddist claptrap on which the vanguardists relied.[57]

Jiménez reserved some of his vitriol for the literary scholars. The common species he considered to be a petty, opportunistic pursuer of minutiae who had no understanding of poetry. To this type, criticism is often a means of venting personal animosity, the practice of "literary politics", adulation of the mediocre who can benefit the adulator, criticism exercised for the critics' gain. Jiménez lamented that many who wish to inform themselves about their own literature or that of another country fill their heads with this marginal trivia instead of going directly to the authors they wish to know. Literature declines as bibliographers multiply. "Happy the times in which there were poets and critics and not bibliographers", exclaimed Jiménez, expressing a sentiment which might be echoed today by the many who have experienced similar frustrations in their contacts with the academic literati.[58]

Jiménez had devoted more than fifty years of his life to writing, and he was fond of reliving some of his experiences in the world of letters. Some of his prose pieces could more properly be called reminiscences or memoirs than literary criticism. As he recalled some writer or scene from the past, his essays, like his conversations, tended to become somewhat rambling, personalized literary chronicles, often in a nostalgic-humorous vein. He had an excellent memory for detail, especially for revealing peculiarities of speech, gesture, bearing, dress, a faculty of which he made effective use when he wrote of friends and associates of other days. The eccentricities and foibles, which he remembered with evident amusement, served to individualize and humanize the figures in this gallery of memoirs.

News of the death of Salvador Rueda in 1933 moved Jiménez to write a tribute to him, which began by acknowledging the influence the older poet had had on his own early work. Jiménez recalls their meeting in 1898, the very day he arrived in Madrid for the first time, then a youth of seventeen. Rueda, a poet of rustic Andalusian antecedents, was forty-one. He had won considerable renown as a "colorist" and metrical innovator. Jiménez' recollections of Rueda are very personal, vivid, amusing but kind: "...He was so kind as to visit me in the Sanatorio del Retraído with his white bricklayer's suit, sometimes a cap and sandals, which 'I wear'—he used to say—'to mingle truly with the (common) people'. The last time I saw him was, I believe—how long ago—in 1903".

As Jiménez remembered him, Rueda resembled an "amiable

cabinetmaker on Sunday'', his complexion somewhere between dark and tawny, eyes half-gay, half-sad, a shock of hair and a big moustache. Rueda walked with short rapid steps, and he turned his whole body when he greeted someone on the street. He had a phobia about crossing town squares, and he never stepped on the line where one section of a sidewalk joined another. His speech was ingratiating and gentle, interspersed with sighs, full of idioms and popular interjections. Rueda prided himself rather childishly on his technical innovations, but Jiménez credited him with having written some unrhymed verses of "rich intuitive beauty", and with having brought "light, intoxication and life" to Spanish poetry, which was "dry as cork" until he appeared.[59] It was fitting that after Rueda's death he should be honored, not with a pompous eulogy, but with this living portrait by Jiménez, to whom he had been an early master, a fellow poet and a friend.

Jiménez wrote in a similar vein of several other literary acquaintances: Rubén Darío, Francisco Villaespesa, Valle Inclán, Ortega y Gasset, to mention only those most widely known.[60] These "essays" combine biography, memoirs and literary criticism. In their surprising recall of subtle but distinguishing traits of personality and physical image, and in their psychological penetration, they resemble the "lyric caricatures". However, their lively, conversational style has the spontaneous flow of *viva voce* reminiscences, unlike the belabored baroque prose of many of the caricatures. These may be more sophisticated, more ingenious, more "literary" than the memoirs, but the sentimental tone, the discursive development and the charitable humor of the latter infuse them with a warmth and humanity that the caricatures generally lack.

CHAPTER 7

Summation

J UAN RAMÓN JIMÉNEZ began his literary career as the nineteenth century was drawing to a close. The Spanish-American War had just ended, and with it the last vestiges of the vast colonial empire over which Spain had once ruled. It was a time of sober reflection and reappraisal. A new generation of intellectuals and writers saw the need of awakening the national conscience and arousing the nation from the complacency which had been the prelude to the disaster of 1898. They envisioned a resurgent Spain, vigorous and creative in every aspect of the national life.

The time could hardly have been more propitious for Jiménez to become known as a writer. A few months spent in Madrid in 1900 were charged with the excitement of participating in the creative movement now under way. The presence of Ruben Darío in Madrid had attracted Jiménez to the city, and to Modernism, the literary fashion of the day. Darío, the literary idol and the most eminent Modernist of Latin America, soon had enthusiastic followers in Spain, among them Jiménez. The acquaintance with Darío, and with the works of the French Symbolists, from whom Modernism was in large part derived, were strong factors in determining the course Jiménez was to follow for more than a decade in his poetic evolution. In 1903 Jiménez published a collection of lyric poems, *Sad Airs,* which showed for the first time that he had passed from the exaggerated sentimentality, the capricious formal experimentation and imitation typical of his early poems, to a surer grasp of his own capabilities, which were soon to produce another meritorious volume, *Pastorals* (1905).

Jiménez spent the years 1905 to 1912 in relative isolation in his native town, Moguer. It was a productive period, in which one volume of poems followed another in rather close succession.

143

Many of the poems of these years are impressionistic in their imagery, somewhat morbid in tone, but they established Jiménez as a lyric poet of unusual sensibility.

From 1912 until the outbreak of the civil war Jiménez lived in Madrid in close contact with Spain's leading men of letters and intellectuals. *Platero and I* (1914), his first book in prose, was enthusiastically received both in Spain and abroad, and in the sixty years elapsed since its first publication it has suffered no decline in popularity. It can justly be called a classic of Spanish literature. *The Diary of a Newly Married Poet,* published shortly after Jiménez' marriage to Zenobia Camprubí, is without doubt the most important poetic work he had written up to this point in his life. This volume marks the beginning of the poet's maturity and of a quest for more transcendent values in poetry and life. By this time Modernism had declined in favor and prestige. The *Diary* represented a new direction in Spanish poetry. It was followed by several other poetic works of high quality: *Eternities, Rock and Sky, Beauty, Poetry (in Verse).* No one could now challenge Jiménez' position and influence in Hispanic poetry.

The twenty-two years Jiménez spent in Spanish America and the United States saw no decline in his creative capabilities—except during his periodic states of depression—nor in the authority of his critical judgment. *Animal of Depth, Desired and Desiring God, Space* show that time—more than a half century—had not dimmed his spiritual and esthetic vision nor wasted his creative vigor. His work never became anachronistic, because he renewed it repeatedly. The Nobel Prize, which he received in 1956, seemed appropriate recognition for the excellence of his work and the many years he had devoted to it.[1] Not since 1920 had the prize gone to a Spanish author. The recipient of that year, Jacinto Benavente, was an old friend, who, with Jiménez had participated in the Spanish literary revival of the early years of the twentieth century.

Zenobia died only two days after word came from Stockholm that Jiménez was to receive the Nobel Prize. The news brought her a few final moments of happiness. Jiménez did not long survive her. Zenobia had been his loving, loyal companion for forty years. Life without her was empty and purposeless. After death they were returned to Spain together, and lie buried side by side in the cemetery of Moguer. Living in other lands, far from Spain, Jiménez felt uprooted, a "Spanish poplar with its roots in the air", as he said. His cultural roots were deep in Spanish tradition, the profound sustaining source of his poetic creation throughout his life. It was a fitting tribute to him that he was brought home at last, with Zenobia, and buried in Spanish soil.

Notes and References

Chapter One

1. *Francisco Garfias, Juan Ramón Jiménez* (Madrid, 1958), pp. 16-22; Graciela Palau de Nemes, *Vida y obra de Juan Ramón Jiménez* (Madrid, 1957), pp. 16-19.

2. In a letter to Rubén Darío, Jiménez commented on the tranquility of life in Moguer, but complained that the town had nothing to offer in the way of museums, concerts or sculpture gardens. See my monograph *The Literary Collaboration and the Personal Correspondence of Rubén Darío and Juan Ramón Jiménez* (Coral Gables, Fla., University of Miami Press 1956), p. 34.

3. Guillermo Diaz-Plaja, *Juan Ramón Jiménez en su poesia* (Madrid, 1958), pp. 25-28.

4. Garfias, p. 23.

5. Carlos del Saz Orozco, *El concepto de Dios en Juan Ramón Jiménez* (Madrid, 1963), p. 16; Palau de Nemes, pp. 25-26.

6. The date of his return to Moguer is not given in any of Jiménez' writings but it was probably late in 1897. Several of his paintings are dated 1897.

7. The word which appears in the text is *ánguila*, obviously a misprint, since *ánguila* is neither fish nor fowl. What Jiménez must have meant is *águila* (eagle). However, it is highly unlikely that a small boy would have had a full grown eagle for a pet, carrying it with him wherever he went; for this reason *"eaglet"* seems the most acceptable translation of *águila*.

8. *Por el cristal amarillo,* ed. Francisco Garfias (Madrid; Aguilar 1961), pp. 263-264.

Chapter Two

1. *El gran galeoto* (The Great Procurer) the best known of Echegaray's plays, was published in 1881. Echegaray was the first Spanish writer to win the Nobel Prize for literature. He was a scientist and politician, a dramatist only by avocation. By the time he died, in 1916, his prestige as an author had greatly declined.

2. Leopoldo Alas, *Paliques* (Madrid: V. Suárez, 1893), p. 273.

3. Charles Fraker, "Bécquer and the Modernists", *Hispanic Review,* III (January, 1935), i, 36-44.

4. Jorge Guillén, *La Poética de Bécquer* (New York: The Hispanic Institute, p. 18.

5. Rubén Darío, *España contemporánea* (Paris: Garnier, 1901), p. 34.

6. Eusebio Blasco, "Vida Nueva", *Vida Nueva, June 12, 1898.*

7. Pedro Salinas, *La Poesía de Rubén Darío* (Buenos Aires: Losada, 1948), p. 122.

8. In *Unión Ibero-Americana* (Ibero-American Union) October 30, 1900.

9. The first poem "Ofertorio" ("Offertory"), as well as six others in *Water Lilies, are obvious metrical imitations of the Nocturne".* See the poems entitled "Tétrica, Gloomy", "Cementerio", (Cemetery), "La cremación del sol", ("The Cremation of the Sun"), "Los amanates del miserable", ("The Lovers of the Wretch"), "Paisaje del corazón", ("Landscape of the Heart"), "Spoliarium", in Juan Ramón Jiménez *Primeros libros de poesía.* Francisco Garfias, ed. (Madrid, 1967), pp. 1478-1479, 1482-1483, 1491-1493, 1495-1496, 1496-1498. Quotations from this volume will be identified by the letters PLP followed by the page number.

10. See Enrique Díiz-Canedo, *Juan Ramón Jiménez en su obra* (Mexico, 1944), p. 38.

11. The article from the Seville newspaper *El Porvenir* was preserved in an undated clipping from Jiménez' personal files. The approximate date of publication: late 1900 or early 1901.

12. Díez-Canedo, p. 38.

13. The term is not necessarily derogatory, although it was often so used. In his early period Jiménez was so intrigued by Modernism that he tended to imitate some of its more censurable aspects as well as the good ones. As examples one might cite "Nocturno" ("Nocturne"), "Tristeza primaveral" ("Spring Sadness"), "El lago del dolor" ("The Lake of Sorrow"). See *Primeros libros de poesía,* pp. 101-103, 137-138, 163-164.

14. See "Recuerdo al primer Villaespesa", *El Sol,* Madrid, May 10, 1936.

15. Some of the titles have been changed, and in a few others minor revisions have been made, but the poems remain essentially the same as in the original versions.

16. *Rhymes* is dedicated to the memory of his father, to his mother, his sisters and brother.

17. Jiménez himself stated that he chose the Sanatorio "in order not to live on city streets but in the country, to which I was completely accustomed...." "El modernismo poética en España e Hispanoamérica", *Revista de América,* VI (Bogotá, April 1946), p. 28.

18. "In this atmosphere of convent and garden I spent two of the best years of my life. Some romantic love of religious sensuality, conventual peace, the smell of incense and flowers, a window over the garden, a terrace with roses for moonlit nights..." quoted by Díez-Canedo, pp. 38-39.

19. Much later in life Jiménez spoke of the "lamentable, silly pessimism" of *Sad Airs,* a more severe judgment of the book than it actually deserved.

20. Ramón Gómez de la Serna, *Retratos contemporáneos (Contemporary Portraits)* (Buenos Aires, 1941), p. 29.

21. Published in Darío's collection of essays, *Tierras Solares,* (Madrid: Editorial Mundo Latino), probable date, 1903.

22. For an interesting and informative account of the work of the Institución Libre de Enseñanza see J. B. Trend, *Origins of Modern Spain,* New York: Macmillan, 1934.

23. According to his own admission, Jiménez had definite Krausist leanings during this period of his life. See Ricardo Gullón, *Conversaciones con Juan Ramón (Conversations With Juan Ramón), (Madrid: Taurus, 1958), pp. 57-58.*

24. *See del Saz Orozco, pp. 127-128.*

25. *Viewing his early work in retrospect Jiménez made the following comment on the first romance he recalled having written (in 1897-1898):* "Did that *romance* (Octosyllabic verse form) come from popular tradition? No doubt, popular tradition was in me like a brook on the way to a river. My blood circulated in *romance,* I could hear it. That was a folk song, cultured because of the unconsciously reflected model of Heine, of Bécquer and of Musset, whose *Intermezzo* and whose *Nights* I was then reading. Musset gave it the seriousness and Heine the second accent". *(Por el cristal amarillo, p. 270).*

Chapter Three

1. *Many years after his first visit to Madrid Jiménez still recalled vividly the rather dismal impression the city had made on him on that occasion. "Recuerdo al primer Villaespesa", El Sol, Madrid, May 10, 1936.*

2. Enrique Díez-Canedo says of *Rhymes,* "The displays of Modernism have disappeared", alluding no doubt more to the versification used in this volume than to the themes and sentiment. *Díez-Canedo,* p. 32.

3. Jiménez was a loyal friend and defender of Darío's at a time when many Spanish readers and critics looked on the Nicaraguan poet as a subverter of Hispanic tradition and of good taste. It was common to blame Darío for whatever sins were committed in the name of Modernism. Darío

answered his critics in an article published in *La Vida literaria* in 1899. Humorous and ironic in tone, the article was nevertheless of serious intent, aimed particularly at those Spaniards who were outraged by the propensity of young Spanish-American poets to seek a more cosmopolitan literary orientation than that which nineteenth-century Spain had to offer. See my book *Españoles de América y americanos de España* (Madrid: Gredos 1968), p. 66.

4.   The literary controversy provoked by Modernism began in the last decade of the nineteenth century but has continued down to the present. Jiménez came to regard Modernism as a sort of contemporary Renaissance embracing not only literature but art, religion, philosophy, esthetics, culture in general. It is obvious that when he spoke of his reaction against Modernism he was using the word in the conventional sense, referring to the superficial innovations that it produced and with which it has often been associated. Thus, in his comment on *Rhymes* it appears that he accepts the conventional view of Modernism, although to him the word actually had a much broader meaning.

5.   Guillermo Díaz-Plaja states that the reaction against Modernism began about 1905. *Modernismo frente a noventa y ocho* (Madrid: Espasa-Calpe 1951, p. 68. *Cantos de vida y esperanza* (1905) initiates what has often been considered a new direction in Darío's poetry and thus "a reaction against Modernism".

6.   This stanza is an adaptation of a stanza from Musset's "Ballade á la lune" which Jiménez had used as an epigraph to his poem. The main difference between the original and Jiménez' version is the use of syllabic rhyme in the latter. I have not translated the stanza because of the impossibility of retaining the syllabic rhyme in the translation.

7.   *Profane Proses* more than any other work of Darío's drew fire from conservative critics, who were in varying degrees outraged by its innovations.

8.   See *La poesía de Rubén Darío,* p. 93.

9.   "Una entrevista con Juan Ramón Jiménez", *La prensa* (New York, February 1, 1953).

10.   Garfias, p. 51.

11.   The dates given are those of publication. In many cases the poems were written two or three years before they were published.

12.   The following stanza from *Labyrinth* is cited as an example:
Everything takes on a strange and unseemly look,
Todo toma un aspecto extraño y de deshora,
as if the world were inverted in a moment,
como si el mundo se invirtiera en un momento,
and one might say things have never been
y las cosas, dijérase que nunca han sido de
any other way, that they have never had more than this.

otro modo, que nunca han tenido más que esto.

(PLP, 1251)

13. The volume is dedicated to José Enrique Rodó, Uruguayan essayist, who enjoyed great prestige in Spain in the early years of the twentieth century. For comment on the contacts between Rodó and Jiménez see my article "La correspondencia entre José Enrique Rodó y Juan Ramón Jiménez, "*Revista Iberoamericana,* XXV, no. 50 (1960), 327-336.

14. Anyone who has read San Juan de la Cruz will recall such examples as the following: "the silent music", "Oh precious wound", "I die because I do not die", "to know unknowing". This type of figure is very common in Jiménez. A great number of examples like the following could be cited: "end without end", "nightfall, eternal dawn", "gleaming darkness", "immortal mortal flower of mine".

15. These verses call to mind a poem by Emily Dickinson, more subtly expressed but inspired by the same sentiment. At the time he wrote *The Sonorous Solitude* Jiménez almost certainly had never heard of the American poetess, who later came to be one of his favorites. Her poem follows:

Presentiment—is that long Shadow—on the Lawn—
Indicative that Suns go down—
The Notice to the startled grass
That Darkness—is about to pass—.

16. Antonio Sánchez-Barbudo, *La segunda época de Juan Ramón Jiménez* (Madrid, 1962), p. 11.

17. "Lucie" begins thus:

My dear friends, when I die
Plant a willow in the cemetery.
I like its weeping foliage,
Its paleness is sweet and dear to me,
and its shade will be light
To the earth where I shall sleep.

18. Sabine R. Ulibarri devotes to this subject an entire chapter of his book *El mundo poético de Juan Ramón Jiménez* (Madrid, 1962), pp. 208-224.

19. Díaz-Plaja, p. 171.

20. This is the theme of one of the closing poems of *Melancholy.* See PLP, 1455.

Chapter Four

1. Palau de Nemes, p. 167.
2. Ramón Gómez de la Serna was particularly insistent that Jiménez

move to Madrid. See Gómez de la Serna, p. 36.

3. The Residencia de Estudiantes was actually a continuation of the Institución Libre de Enseñanza founded by Francisco Giner and Manual Cossío. The same tolerance, enthusiasm and devotion to culture prevailed in the Residencia as in the earlier institution. See Rafael Alberti, *Imagen primera de Juan Ramón Jiménez* (et al.) (Buenos Aires, 1945), pp. 15-22.

4. The "Nobel Prize edition" of Jiménez' poetic works, *Libros de Poesía* (Madrid, 1959) begins with *Spiritual Sonnets* and includes all of the later books of poetry except the anthologies. Quotations from this volume will be identified by the letters LP followed by the page number of the quotation and—except where already identified—the title of the original book, e.g. (LP, 25, *Summer*).

5. The sonnet "a mi pena" ("to my grief") contains an irregularity in the fourth verse of the second stanza. This line contains twelve rather than the de rigueur eleven syllables:

> Te salía tu aroma por doquiera,
> esencia nueva, que al resplandeciente
> dia le era su olor propio y conciente...
> Llegada la última, fuiste la primera.
> (LP, 61)

Jiménez used enjambement occasionally to join one stanza to another, a kind of overflowing of one into the next without altering the syllabic content of the whole. For an example, see "El corazón roto" ("The Broken Heart") (LP, 30).

6. The sonnet "Mujer celeste" exemplifies this tendency (LP, 27).

7. My italics.

8. See Gerardo Diego, "Estío", *Revista de Occidente,* I (1923), 366; Díaz-Plaja, p. 213.

9. The early editions all bore this title, but in 1948 a revised edition was prepared by Jiménez and published in Buenos Aires under the title *Diary of the Poet and the Sea (Diario de poeta y mar).*

10. Jiménez made the statement in an article which attributed to the *Diary* a major influence in contemporary Hispanic poetry. See "El modernismo poético", *Revista de América,* VI, (Bogotá, April 1946), p. 28.

11. See Sánchez-Barbudo, *La segunda época* p. 57, note 17.

12. As an example of a composition in which the sublime and the sordid are in juxtaposition one might cite "La negra y la rosa" ("The Negress and the Rose", LP, 327-328). Here the poet forgets the sordidness of the subway as he observes a sleeping woman holding a white rose in her hand. Another example: "Viva la Primavera" ("Long Live Spring") LP, 361-362.

13. Huidobro is generally recognized in Spanish America as the founder of Creationism, although the French poet, Pierre Reverdy, made

the same claim for himself. Huidobro lived in France from 1916 to 1925, maintained close relations with the vanguard poets of France and published several poetic works in French. He visited Madrid in 1918, where his poetic theories were enthusiastically received by many of the young writers of Spain, and gave impetus to Ultraism, the country's leading vanguard movement of the day. Jiménez kept at a discreet distance from the many "isms" then flourishing, although it is apparent that his thinking in at least one respect paralleled that of the Creationists.

14. Sánchez-Barbudo, pp. 71-72.

15. The haiku enjoyed some prestige and popularity in the Hispanic world during the twenties. The Mexican poet José Juan Tablada, noted for his "Nipponophilia", claimed to have been the first Hispanic cultivator of the haiku, whose vogue began around 1920.

16. The first of these contains only two verses: "Touch it no more / for thus is the rose" ("No le toques ya más / que así es la rosa"), but it is one of the best known and most often quoted poems of Jiménez.

17. There is a poem in *Green Leaves* in which Jiménez addresses this question to the moon: "Did Jesus Christ also trouble your pleasures?" ("¿También turbó tus placeres, Jesu Cristo?") (PLP, 719).

18. Carlos del Saz Orozco has given a complete exposition of Jiménez' religious thinking in his book *God in Juàn Ramón.*

19. As a translator of Tagore, in collaboration with Zenobia, Jiménez must have had ample occasion to explore Hindu religious thought.

20. *World Bible,* ed. Robert O. Ballou (New York: Viking Press, 1966), p. 28.

21. Palau de Nemes, pp. 240-245.

22. Alberti, p. 35.

23. See "Gongorismo", *Esthetics and Esthetic Ethics,* ed. Francisco Garfias (Madrid, 1967), pp. 25-26.

24. In a conversation I once had with Cernuda he criticized Jiménez with some bitterness for his harsh judgment of the Spanish poets of the day. He characterized Jiménez as being "allergic to Spanish poets".

25. Alberti, p. 37.

26. Alfonso Reyes, *Tertulia en Madrid* (Buenos Aires: Losado, 1922), p. 49.

27. *Introducción a la poesía española contemporánea* (Madrid: Guadarrama, 1957), p. 51.

Chapter Five

1. Luis Cernuda, *Estudios sobre poesía española contemporánea* (Madrid, 1957), p. 134.

2. Published by the Institución Hispanocubana de Cultura, Havana, 1937.

3. The question is, of course, open to debate. Some might consider García Lorca, Pablo Neruda or Antonio Machado of wider influence than Jiménez.

4. Eduardo Cote Lamus, "La última poesía colombiana", *Primeras jornadas de lengua y literatura colombianas* (Salamanca), 1956.

5. Other well-known members of the group were Aurelio Arturo, Antonio Llanos, Tomás Vargas Osorio, Gerardo Valencia and Carlos Martin.

6. The "Contemporáneos" were all contributors to the prestigious literary review of the same name, published between 1928-1931. The group included Bernardo Ortiz de Montellano, Jaime Torres Bodet, José Gorostiza, Xavier Villaurrutia, Salvador Novo, Jorge Cuesta and others. Carlos Pellicer is also usually included, although some regard him as independent of the group.

7. *Obras escogidas de Jaime Torres Bodet* (México: Fondo de Cultura Económica, 1961), p. 294.

8. Villaurrutia was, like Jiménez, an esthete and a metaphysical poet.

9. "Lamentaciones de primavera", *Poesía y teatro completos de Xavier Villaurrutia* (México: Fondo de Cultura Económica, 1953), p. 5. For another example, see "Espejo" (*Poesía y teatro,* p. 29), a poem very similar, both in theme and expression, to many of Jiménez' short lyrics.

10. José Gorostiza, *Poesía* (México: Fondo de Cultura Económica, 1964), pp. 76-77.

11. Paz credits Jiménez with having written his best poetry in his old age. He is particularly impressed by *Espacio* (*Space*), and it is quite possible this work contributed something to Paz' poetic evolution in recent years. The Mexican critic considers *Space* a major work of modern poetry. *El arco y la lira* (México: Fondo de Cultura Económica, 1970), pp. 95-96.

12. "Palabra", *Libertad bajo palabra* (México: Fondo de Cultura Económica, 1970, p. 31.

13. See Chapter IV, p. 72 . Howard Young sees this poem as a manifestation of Jiménez' impulse toward "pure" poetry. *The Victorious Expression* (Madison, 1966), p. 108.

14. Jiménez stated it thus: "Written poetry seems to me, always continues to seem to me that it is the expression (like the musical, etc.; of the ineffable...." "Poesía y literatura", *University of Miami Hispanic-American Studies* (Coral Gables, Florida, 1941), no. 2, p. 75.

15. Max Henríquz Ureña mentions several Peruvian poets visibly influenced by Jiménez: José Gálvez, Adán Espinosa Saldaña, Alberto J. Ureta. Another he does not mention, but whose early work may have been considerably influenced by Jiménez, is Enrique Bustamente Ballivián. See Augusto Tamayo Vargas, "Cincuenta años de poesía peruana", *Revista Hispánica Moderna,* April-October 1962, pp. 304-314. Ureña states that in Chile the Jiménez line continues in the poetry of Jorge González Bastías.

The Return of the Galleons (Madrid: Artes gráficas, 1930), p. 55.

It is quite likely that in their poetic formation both Huidobro and Neruda owed something to Jiménez, although both of them diverged widely from him in their subsequent evolution. Jiménez declared that Neruda imitated him in his early works, *Crepusculario* and *Veinte canciones de amor* (*Twenty Songs of Love*). See Gullón, *Conversaciones*, p. 54. Whether Jiménez' claim was accurate or not seems unimportant. What may be more significant is that in some of his poems—although certainly not the majority—there is something akin to the *feísmo* of Neruda's *Residencias*. This type of imagery occurs particularly in the period of *Melancholy* (around 1911 or 1912), but it can be found also in some later works. There is no reason to doubt that Neruda had read these works of Jiménez before he wrote the *Residencias*. In them the Chilean poet may have found some encouragement to follow what seemed to be his natural bent.

The publication of *Animal of Depth* in 1949, after Jiménez' lectures and personal contacts with writers in Argentina and Uruguay, was followed by a a religious reaction in the poetry of those countries, particularly among the younger poets, although not exclusively so. Francisco Luis Bernárdez, already in his maturity, was, of course, already widely known for his lyrics of religious inspiration. The title of one of his collections, *Sky of Earth,* may have been suggested by *Piedra y cielo* (*Rock and Sky*). Bernárdez, much more orthodox than Jiménez in his expression of religious sentiment, was, like Jiménez, a spiritual descendant of San Juan de la Cruz.

In *Azor* (1953), a collection of poems by the once celebrated, although now infrequently mentioned, Juana de Ibarbourou, there is a poem in two parts titled "Así es la rosa", from the initial poem of *Rock and Sky,* well known to all Jiménez readers: "¡no le toques ya más, / que así es la rosa!" The final stanza mentions the poet by his familiar name "Juan Ramón".

16. The Jiménez remained in Cuba until 1939, then moved to Miami, where they made their home until 1942. From the latter date until 1951 they lived in Washington, D. C. or the adjacent suburban area in Maryland. In 1951, plagued by ill health and mental depression, the poet, accompanied by his devoted Zenobia, sought refuge again in Puerto Rico. There Jiménez remained the rest of his life.

17. J. B. Trend's *Fifty Spanish Poems*, a collection of Jiménez' poems with English translations, published by the University of California Press, appeared in 1951. *Poetry* devoted an entire number to selections from Jiménez' poetry and prose with translations by W. S. Merwin, Rachel Frank and Julia Howe. *Poetry,* LXXXII, no. 4 (1953). However, it was not until 1956, the year Jiménez won the Nobel Prize, that any substantial volumes of American translations, such as the following, began to appear: *The Selected Writings of Juan Ramón Jiménez,* trans. H. R. Hays, introd.

Eugenio Florit (New York, 1953); *Platero and I,* trans William and Mary Roberts, illus. Baltasar Lobo (Oxford, 1956); *Platero and I,* trans. Eloise Roach, illus. Jo Alyo Downs (Austin, 1957).

18.   These poems were written during the years Jiménez lived in Coral Gables, but they were not published until 1948.

19.   Palau de Nemes, p. 318. Ricardo Gullón, *El último Juan Ramón* (Madrid, Alfaguara, 1968), p. 17.

20.   Jiménez wrote a laudatory personal sketch of Wallace. See "Henry A. Wallace, el mejor", *La corriente infinita,* ed. Francisco Garfias (Madrid: Aguilar, 1961), pp. 201-207.

21.   Díez-Canedo, p. 139.

22.   Mexico: Editorial Stylo, 1948.

23.   Guillermo Díaz-Plaja comments that the old poems in *Voices of My Song* are similar in style and content to the new poems, which contributes to the unity of the collection. *Díaz-Plaja,* p. 281. It appears that the author had not discovered that *all* of these poems, without exception, were taken from earlier works. The volume contained no new poems.

24.   Buenos Aires: Losada, 1946.

25.   *Romance* is the traditional Spanish octosyllabic verse, not the equivalent of the English word "romance". "Ballad" is only an approximation of the Spanish word *romance.*

26.   The book is divided into three parts; the first and third both bear the title "Total Season". The second part is made up of twenty-six brief poems, nearly all previously published in *Song,* and reappearing now under the title "Songs of the New Light". The publication date, 1946, is much later than the dates of composition, 1923-1936, given under the title.

27.   *Díaz-Plaja,* p. 294.

28.   The verse is awkward in translation. The accurate rendering of the meaning may suggest things to the English-speaking reader that would not occur to the Spanish reader. *Alma,* which Jiménez uses frequently, can only be translated "soul", a word which might strike many contemporary American readers as hackneyed and Victorian. They would be more disposed than the Spanish reader to conclude that the poem in which it is used is pedestrian, its language impoverished or outmoded.

29.   See Bertrand Russell, *A History of Western Philosophy* (New York: Simon and Shuster, 1960), p. 290.

30.   Antonio Sánchez-Barbudo, to cite one example, makes the following comment on one of the poems of *Total Season:* "In some of the poems the narcissistic Juan Ramón reappears, satisfied with himself, eager to be self sufficient. The best example is the little poem entitled, precisely, "Example" in which he is the example...." *La segunda época,* p. 120.

31.   Walter Pattison calls Jiménez a "mystic of nature". *Hispania,* XXIII (1950), 18-22. Luis Vivanco refers to him as a "mystic of beauty". *Introducción a la poesía española contemporánea* (Madrid: Guadarrama,

1957), p. 60.

32. Vivanco, p. 58.

33. Sánchez-Barbudo comments that death is scarcely mentioned in *Total Season. La segunda época,* p. 118.

34. Other poems of affirmation of the new reality are "Lo que sigue" ("What Follows") (LP, 1138), "El Oasis" ("The Oasis") (LP, 1160), "Su sitio Fiel" ("Its Faithful Place") (LP, 1170), "Mirlo fiel" ("Faithful Blackbird") (LP, 1261-1262), "El viento mejor" ("The Best Wind") (LP, 1281), "Mensajero de la estacíon total" ("Messenger of the Total Season") (LP, 1282-1283).

35. Octavio Paz, *El arco y la lira* (México: Fondo de Cultura Económica, 1970), pp. 21-22.

36. Vivanco, p. 70.

37. *Poesía y mística en Juan Ramón Jiménez* (Santiago, 1969), p. 214.

38. Sánchez-Barbudo states it thus: "The 'messenger' is at once the grace, the external world touched by that light of grace, and the soul of the poet, from which all comes, since as he says on other occasions, everything takes place in the 'immanence' within him" (*La segunda época,* p. 134.

39. The *Ballads of Coral Gables* are not included in *Libros de Poesía*. The quotations from the former are taken from the following edition: *Romances de Coral Gables* (México, 1948).

40. Paul Olson, *Circle of Paradox: Time and Essence in the Poetry of Juan Ramón Jiménez* (Baltimore, 1967), p. 121.

41. The translation used here is that of Paul Olson, *Circle of Paradox,* p. 122.

42. For a more extensive commentary on this poem see Sánchez-Barbudo, *Cincuenta poemas comentados* (Madrid: Gredos, 1963), pp. 142-146.

43. For details of the composition and publication of *Space* see Howard T. Young, "Génesis y forma de 'Espacio' de Juan Ramón Jiménez", *Revista Hispánica Moderna,* XXXIV, nos. 1-2 (1968), 462-470.

44. It will be remembered that in "The Poetic Principle" Poe stated "I hold that a long poem does not exist....I need scarcely observe that a poem deserves its title only inasmuch as it excites by elevating the soul....That degree of excitement which would entitle a poem to be so called at all, cannot be sustained throughout a composition of any great length...." *The Works of Edgar Allan Poe,* ed. R. Brimley Johnson (London, 1927), p. 167.

45. Palau de Nemes, p. 316.

46. Jiménez esteemed Edwin Arlington Robinson as a poet, and sometimes mentioned him in his writings and his conversations. However, it is hardly conceivable that such a totally different work as *Tristram* could have had any connection with the conception of *Space*.

47. Unamuno's *El Cristo de Velázquez* (1920); Huidobro's *Altazor*

(1931); Neruda's *Tentativa del hombre infinito* (1925) and *Residencia I* (1933), *II* (1937); and Gorostiza's *Muerte sin fin* (1938).

48. Jiménez was more than twenty years older than Neruda and Gorostiza, twelve years older than Huidobro. Unamuno was Jiménez' senior by seventeen years.

49. For the Spanish text see *Third Poetic Anthology* (*Tercera antología poética*) (Madrid, 1957), pp. 851-852. Quotations from this book will be identified by the letters TA followed by the page number.

50. The nightingale, of course, does not exist in Florida. What Jiménez refers to repeatedly in *Space* is the mocking bird, which abounds in Florida. Despite the unpoetic name it bears, the mocking bird rivals the nightingale in virtuosity and may even surpass it in endurance. In its native habitat, which embraces Florida, it can be heard both night and day in certain seasons.

51. Díez-Canedo, p. 140.

52. In *Space* Jiménez, like Kant, sees time and space as subjective. For example, he says "What was this morning no longer is, nor has it been except in me" ("Lo que fué esta mañana ya no es, ni ha sido más que en mí") (TA, 856).

53. Del Saz Orozco, p. 143.

54. See, for example, Francisco López Estrada, "En el tercer camino", *Clavileño,* Madrid (1953), no. 23, p. 51.

55. Rinaldo Froldi makes the following comment on *Animal of Depth:* "*Animal of Depth* is the point of arrival of Jiménez' long poetic journey; it seems almost to be the definitive end of an activity which lasted more than fifty years for the conquest of poetry. This is why *Animal of Depth* cannot be understood without the production which precedes it. One needs to feel it in the unity of all the poetry of Juan Ramón." The translated quotation is from "Introduzione", *Animale di fondo* (Firenze: Edizioni di Revoluzioni, 1954), p. 9.

56. This quotation is from the Notes (Notas) appended to *Animal of Depth* in *Libros de poesía,* p. 1343.

57. Ricardo Gullón, *Estudios sobre Juan Ramón Jiménez* (Buenos Aires: Losada, 1960), p. 145.

58. One of the many coined words which Jiménez uses in *Animal of Depth.*

59. Jiménez might have called the *Diary* "my first sea" since it was inspired by his ocean journey to New York and back to Spain, after his marriage to Zenobia. His "second sea", his last East-West crossing of the Atlantic, produced no new volume of poetry. The "third sea" refers to the journey to Argentina and Uruguay and the trip back to the United States, which inspired *Animal of Depth.*

Jiménez makes the following comment on the genesis of the two poetic works mentioned here: "...My renewal begins at the time of the trip to

America and manifests itself with the *Diary*. The sea makes me live again, because it is the contact with the natural (world), with the elements, and thanks to it abstract poetry comes. Thus the *Diary* is born, and many years later, thanks also to the sea, on the occasion of the trip to Argentina, *Desired and Desiring God* comes forth". Quoted by Gullón in *Conversaciones*, p. 120.

60. Sánchez-Barbudo, *La segunda época,* pp. 196-197.

61. Del Saz Orozoco, pp. 211-215.

62. Lira, p. 230.

63. *Ibid.,* p. 232.

64. Paul Olson has commented on a type of paradox which Jiménez has "borrowed directly" from San Juan de la Cruz. *Circle of Paradox,* p. 30. The paradox was certainly one of his favorite rhetorical devices.

65. I have tried to approximate Jiménez' coined words by using the Latin prefix *ultra*—common to both languages—combining it with the nouns *sea, land, sky,* just as Jiménez does with the corresponding Spanish words.

66. Sánchez-Barbudo comments quite appropriately: "There is perhaps too much word play in this poem, too much south, silver and ultrasea. All to say about the same that he had said other times." *Dios deseado y deseante,* ed. A. Sánchez-Barbudo (Madrid: Aguilar, 1964), p. 111.

67. Concha Zardoya, *Poesía española contemporánea* (Madrid: 1961), p. 238; Gullón, *Estudios,* p. 140.

68. Jiménez persisted in his belief that the *Diary* was his best work. See Gullón, *Conversaciones,* p. 92.

69. Jiménez stated that *Desired and Desiring God* and *Animal of Depth* would together consist of eighty poems. See Gullón, *Conversaciones,* p. 119. Although he never reached this number, those he did compose have been collected, annotated and published. This commendable work of scholarship was performed by Professor Antonio Sánchez-Barbudo of the University of Wisconsin, who has published the complete poems of *Animal of Depth* and the reconstructed sequel under the title *Dios deseado y deseante* (Desired and Desiring God). A prologue precedes the poems, each of which is followed by an explanatory comment. The volume also contains a hitherto unpublished prologue which Jiménez had written for *Desired and Desiring God*. The prologue, entitled "Camino de fe" ("The Way of Faith"), is perhaps the most lucid statement Jiménez ever made concerning his religious views.

70. Published in *Tercera antología poética* (Madrid, 1957).

71. *Dios deseado y deseante,* p. 193. Quotations from this volume will be identified by DD followed by the page number.

72. Martí expressed this wish in a poem (no. XXIII), of *Versos sencillos (Simple Verses)*. Martí was one of the Spanish-American poets

Jiménez most revered and by whom he was unquestionably influenced.

73. *The Gospel According to Saint Mark* 10:15.

74. Sánchez-Barbudo states that in the original manuscript "dios" appeared in the second verse of the poem, but above the "d" Jiménez had written "D" (DD, 266).

75. The complete prologue with explanatory notes by Professor Sánchez-Barbudo is appended to the poems and commentaries in *Dios deseado y deseante,* pp. 225-238.

76. *Ibid.,* pp. 228-229.

77. *Ibid.,* p. 231.

78. This incident was related to me by Zenobia, very soon after it occurred. It amused her more than it disturbed her.

79. The source of this information is, according to Father Lira, an article published by Francisco Hernández Pinzón y Jiménez in a magazine *Incunable,* published in Salamanca. He gives no date. Lira, pp. 217-218 footnote.

80. Gullón, *El último Juan Ramón (The Last Juan Ramón),* p. 171.

81. Sánchez-Barbudo, *La segunda época,* p. 204.

Chapter Six

1. Francisco Garfias, himself a native of Moguer, undertook the collecting and editing of Jiménez' prose for the Aguilar publishing house of Madrid. The content and title of each of the following volumes were selected by Garfias, who also wrote a prologue for each: *Libros de prosa (Books of Prose)* (1969), *La corriente infinita (The Infinite Current)* (1961), *El trabajo gustso (Enjoyable Work)* (1961), *Por el cristal amarillo (Through the Yellow Glass)* (1961), *Estética y ética estética (Esthetics and Esthetic Ethics)* (1967). The volume *Cartas de Juan Ramón Jiménez* (1962) contains letters written by Jiménez, the earliest dated 1898, and the latest, 1958. *Cuadernos de Juan Ramón Jiménez* (1960) contains both poetry and prose previously published in his series of *cuadernos* (notebooks) between 1925 and 1935. Two works edited by Ricardo Gullón contain prose fragments by Jiménez, *Conversaciones con Juan Ramón* (1958) and *El Modernismo* (1962). However, these books were not written *by* Jiménez but are an attempt to record what he said in conversations and lectures. Although Garfias deserves commendation for collecting Jiménez' prose and making it accessible to the public, his scholarship is not thorough; it leaves many questions unanswered.

In 1966 Michael Predmore noted that no one had bothered to write a book on Jiménez' prose, a deficiency which he remedied with his publication of *La obra en prosa de Juan Ramón Jiménez* (Madrid, 1966).

2. These include French, German, Italian (three translations),

Portuguese, Swedish, Norwegian, Dutch, Basque and Hebrew. Two American translations exist, one by William and Mary Roberts (Oxford, 1956), the other by Eloise Roach (Austin, 1957).

3. *Winesburg, Ohio* (1922) was published eight years after the first edition of *Platero*.

4. *Nilda Elena Broggini, Platero y yo, estudio estilístico* (Buenos Aires, 1963).

5. Michael Predmore comments at some length on this aspect of Platero. *La obra en Prosa,* p. 107.

6. When asked whether Platero had existed in real life Jiménez declared that he had indeed existed. He explained that in Andalusia the word *platero* is actually used popularly to classify or describe donkeys of a silvery color. "In reality", he said, "my Platero is not one donkey only but several (in one), a synthesis of *platero* donkeys. As a boy and a young man I had several of them. All were *plateros*. The sum of all my memories with them gave me the creature and the book." Quoted by Francisco Garfias in his Prologue to *Libros de prosa,* p. 25.

7. Jammes' poem "Priére pour aller au Paradis avec les ânes" ends with an entreaty to God that he be allowed to accompany the humble and gentle donkeys when they appear before Him in paradise. *Le deuil des primevères* (Paris, Mercure de France, 1920), pp. 185-187.

8. From the translation by William and Mary Roberts, p. 156. All quotations used in this chapter are from the Roberts' translation.

9. I have translated the following from Jammes' text in French: "...Little donkey, you are my brother. They say you are stupid because you are incapable of doing wrong. You take little steps. When you walk you seem to be thinking this: 'Look! I can't go any faster....Poor people use me because one doesn't give me much to eat'. Little donkey, the goad pricks you. Then you go a little faster, but not much. You can't do any more....You fall down sometimes. Then they beat you, they pull on the rope fastened to your mouth, so hard that your gums turn upward showing your poor yellow teeth, nibblers of wretchedness." *Le roman du liévre* (Paris: Mercure de France, 1927), p. 274.

10. *Platero and I,* pp. 80-81.

11. *Ibid.,* p. 112.

12. *Ibid.,* pp. 47-48.

13. Among those who have commented on this aspect of *Platero and I* are Michael Predmore (*La obra en prosa,* p. 102), Guillermo Díaz-Plaja (p. 190) and Graciela Palau de Nemes (pp. 165-166).

14. I remember a revealing comment Jiménez once made in a casual conversation about another writer, a paralytic who in spite of her disability had won considerable literary recognition. The poet said that humans are nearly always moved emotionally by handicapped persons and by those who have had to endure some adversity or misfortune not normally a part

of human experience. However, the arrogance and harshness of the writer concerned aroused antipathy in those around her, thus stifling the sympathy they would otherwise have felt for her.

15. *Platero and I*, p. 23.

16. *Ibid.*, pp. 150-151.

17. *Ibid.*, pp. 96-97.

18. Mention has already been made of the affinity Jiménez felt toward Baudelaire during one stage of his development. See Chapter Two.

19. Ricardo Gullón finds three levels of meaning in *Platero*: the esthetic, that of reference to Andalusian reality, and that of the human in general. Of Platero and his master he says: "Platero and the poet symbolize the intimate relationship between man and nature, one resting on the other and each understanding the other without words...." Gullón, *Estudios*, p. 121.

20. *Platero and I*, p. 49.

21. *Ibid.*, p. 105.

22. Raimundo Lida, Emmy Nedderman and some others have devoted considerable attention to this aspect of Jiménez' poetry. See Lida, "Sobre el estilo de Juan Ramón Jiménez", *Nosotros* (Buenos Aires, 1937), p. 18; Nedderman, "Juan Ramón Jiménez, sus vivencias y sus tendencias simbolistas", *Nosotros* (Buenos Aires, April 1936), p. 20. Michael Predmore, an exception among the critics of *Platero and I*, takes notice of the impressionism in this work. *La obra en prosa*, pp. 121-122. What requires some qualification is Predmore's statement, "The color, the rhyme, and the musical quality have almost disappeared". *Ibid.*, p. 104. The first and the last of these are still very much in evidence.

23. *Platero and I*, p. 34.

24. *Ibid.*, p. 114.

25. *Ibid.*, p. 91.

26. *Ibid.*, p. 85.

27. *Ibid.*, p. 26.

28. The statement is contained in a prologue written for *Platero y yo*. See the 1963 edition (Madrid: Taurus), pp. 9-10.

29. The three worlds to which Jiménez referred were Spain, Spanish America and the "other" world, i.e., death, since some of the caricatures were of persons no longer living.

30. Gullón, p. 120.

31. As Jiménez states in the prologue, it was his intention to publish a more complete book of caricatures, to number one-hundred-and-fifty in all.

32. Although *Spaniards of Three Worlds* was first published in 1942, the individual sketches began to appear in newspapers and magazines nearly twenty years earlier. The latest in composition date from about 1940.

33. *Españoles de tres mundos* (Buenos Aires, 1942), pp. 21-22.

34. Predmore, *La obra en prosa,* p. 207.

35. Of this feature of *Spaniards of Three Worlds* Jean-Louis Schonberg comments: "It is the burial of the nude under the cauliflowers". *Juan Ramón Jiménez, ou le chant d'Orphée* (Neuchâtel, 1961), p. 174.

36. *Españoles de tres mundos,* p. 123.

37. *Gullón,* Estudios, p. 217. Michael Predmore is equally laudatory in his comments on *Spaniards of Three Worlds.* He considers the work "una verdadera obra maestra".

38. Schonberg, p. 171.

39. María Antonia Salgado has studied the origins of literary caricature, and Jémenez' contribution to the genre. She concludes that Jiménez is unique among Spanish satirists of the twentieth century because of the high lyric quality of his caricatures. *El arte polifacético de las "Caricaturas líricas" juanramonianas* (Madrid, 1968).

40. Jiménez' most important critical articles are the following: "Poesía y literatura", *University of Miami Hispanic-American Studies* (Coral Gables, Florida, 1941), no. 2, pp. 93-107; Crisis del espíritu en la poesía española contemporánea", *Nosotros* (Buenos Aires, 1940), XII, no. 48-49, pp. 165-182; "Poesía cerrada y poesía abierta", *La Torre* (San Juan, Puerto Rico, 1953), I, no. 1, pp. 21-49; "El modernismo poético en España y en Hispanoamérica", *Revista de América,* (Bogotá, 1946), pp. 17-30; "Dos aspectos de Bécquer (Poeta y Crítico)", *Revista de América,* VI, (Bogotá 1946), pp. 145-153; "El único estilo de Eugenio Florit", *Revista Cubana* (La Habana, 1937), VIII, pp. 10-16; "Recuerdo a José Ortega y Gasset", *Claviléno* (Madrid, 1953), no. 24, pp. 44-49; "Recuerdo al primer Villaespesa", *El Sol* (Madrid), 10 de mayo de 1936; "Ramón del Valle-Inclán", *El Sol* (Madrid), 26 de enero de 1936; "El colorista nacional", *El Sol* (Madrid), 30 de mayo de 1933; "Estado poético cubano", prologue to *La poesía cubana en 1936* (La Habana: P. Fernández y Cia, 1937), pp. XII-XXI; "El Romance, Río de la lengua española", in *El trabajo gustoso,* ed. by Francisco Garfias (Madrid: Aguilar, 1961), pp. 143-187. In the preceding list I have given the original place and date of publication of each of the articles by Jiménez. Some of them have appeared in more than one journal or newspaper.

41. "The lucidity of his critical perception was extraordinary. It would not be exaggerated to consider Juan Ramón *when not emotionally upset* (my italics), as one of the keenest critics of our time; a portrait of him which aspires to be complete will have to capture this aspect of his personality, diminished by the splendor of his lyric poetry. In conversations and writings, letters and lectures, he has given evidence of rare sagacity and competence". Gullón, *Estudios,* p. 32.

42. "Poesía y literatura", p. 75.

43. *Ibid.,* p. 78.
44. *Ibid.,* p. 76.
45. *Ibid.,* p. 18.
46. For a comment by Jiménez on the popular element in his own poetry see *Por el cristal amarillo,* p. 270.
47. "Poesía y literatura", p. 79.
48. Leo R. Cole compares the two poets, pointing out important similarities as well as differences. *The Religious Instinct in the Poetry of Juan Ramón Jiménez* (Oxford, 1967), pp. 148-152.
49. "Poesía y literatura", p. 88.
50. "...Bécquer's rhymes had not yet been collected in a book (just as the Songs of his *peer* (my italics) San Juan de la Cruz were not published until rather long after his death). The work of Bécquer, mystic and free, if any (work) is, bears a close relationship to that of the most free and open Spanish mystic..." "Dos aspectos de Bécquer", p. 49.
51. "...This relationship of Unamuno and Darío to Bécquer is fundamental, and it must never be forgotten, because it is the key to many future clarifications, since, in reality, contemporary Spanish poetry begins, without any doubt, with Bécquer". "Crisis del espíritu en la poesía contemporánea", *Estética y ética estética,* ed. F. Garfias (Madrid: Aguilar, 1967), p. 152.
52. To Jiménez, Modernism had a much broader meaning than to most of those who participated in the movement or wrote about it. He saw it as a general cultural renascence, not simply a literary tendency. Others considered it, if not totally dead, to have been submerged by the wave of vanguardism that swept over the Western world during World War I and immediately after it. To Jiménez, Modernism was still alive and vigorous at midcentury. "Crisis del espíritu," pp. 153-154.
53. See my book *Españoles de América y americanos de España* (Madrid: Gredos, 1968), pp. 79-81.
54. "Crisis del espíritu", p. 154.
55. Jiménez lamented that after the Spanish civil war both Spanish and foreign critics exalted what he considered Machado's worst poetry, the more objective and philosophical poems, the Castilian Machado, rather than the lyric and metaphysical Machado. See "Un enredador enredado", *La corriente infinita,* pp. 133-140. This article was first published in the Mexican journal, *Cuadernos Americanos,* July-August, 1944.
56. "Crisis del espíritu", p. 155.
57. *Ibid.,* pp. 163-164.
58. *Ibid.,* pp. 167-168.
59. *La corriente infinita,* p. 57.
60. The prose collection *La corriente infinita* contains essays on the authors named. Several of them were written for the Madrid Newspaper, *El Sol.*

Summation

1. The candidacy of Jiménez for the Nobel Prize was actively supported in Sweden by Ernesto Dethorey, a Spanish journalist who had long resided in Sweden and had published articles on Jiménez in Swedish journals and newspapers. Other important support came from Dr. Arne Häggquist, translator of *Diary of a Newly Married Poet* (1955) and *Platero and I* (1956), and from Hjalmar Gullberg, a well-known poet, member of the Swedish Academy and translator of the poetry of Gabriela, Mistral and Juan Ramón Jiménez. In the spring of 1955 a faculty representative of the University of California addressed a letter to the Secretary of the Swedish Academy recommending Jiménez for the Nobel Prize. At the University of Maryland, Professor Graciela Palau de Nemes took the initiative in enlisting the support of that university for the nomination of Jiménez for the prize. Nominations may also have come from other countries than the United States.

Selected Bibliography

PRIMARY SOURCES

Almas de violeta. Madrid: Tipografía Moderna, 1900.
Ninfeas. Madrid: Tipografía Moderna, 1900.
Rimas. Madrid: Librería Fernando Fe, 1903.
'Arias tristes. Madrid: Fernando Fe, 1903.
Jardines lejanos. Jardines galantes. Jardines místicos. Jardines dolientes.
      Madrid: Fernando Fe, 1904.
Pastorales. Madrid: Renacimiento, 1905.
Olvidanzas. Las hojas verdes. Madrid: Revista de Archivos, 1906.
Elegías puras. Madrid: Revista de Archivos, 1908.
Elegías intermedias. Madrid: Revista de Archivos, 1909
Elegías lamentables. Madrid: Revista de Archivos, 1910.
Baladas de primavera. Madrid: Revista de Archivos, 1910.
La soledad sonora. Madrid: Revista de Archivos, 1911.
Poemas mágicos y dolientes. Madrid: Revista de Archivos, 1911.
Melancolía. Madrid: Revista de Archivos, 1912.
Laberinto. Madrid: Renacimiento, 1913.
Platero y yo. Madrid: La Lectura, 1914.
Estío. Madrid: Calleja, 1916.
Sonetos espirituales. Madrid: Calleja, 1917.
Platero y yo. Madrid: Calleja, 1917. Contains many prose poems not in the
      original edition.
Diario de un poeta recién casado. Madrid: Calleja, 1917.
Poesías escogidas. Madrid: Fortanet, 1917. (New York, The Hispanic
      Society of America.)
Eternidades. Madrid: Calleja, 1918.
Piedra y cielo. Madrid: Fortanet, 1919.
Segunda antología poética. Madrid: Colleción Universal Calpe, 1922.
Belleza. Madrid: Talleres Poligráficos, 1923.
Poesía (en verso). Madrid: Talleres Poligráficos, 1923.
Unidad. Madrid: Sánchez Cuesta, 1929.
Sucesión. 1, 2, 3, 4. Madrid, 1932.
Presente. Madrid: Aguirre, 1933.
Canción. Madrid: Signo, 1936.

Españoles de tres mundos. Buenos Aires: Losada, 1942.
Voces de mi copla. Mexico: Stylo, 1945.
La estación total. Buenos Aires: Losada, 1946.
Romances de Coral Gables. Mexico: Stylo, 1948.
Diario de poeta y mar. Buenos Aires: Losada, 1948. A revised edition of
    Diario de un poeta recién casado.
Animal de fondo. Buenos Aires: Pleamar, 1949. With a French translation
    by Lysandro Z. D. Galtier.
Tercera antología poética. Madrid: Biblioteca Nueva, 1957.
Libros de poesía. Madrid: Aguilar, 1959. The Nobel Prize series. Contains
    the poetic works from *Sonetos espirituales* to *Animal de fondo*,
    including both.
Cartas. Francisco Garfias, ed. Madrid: Aguilar, 1962. Contains letters
    written by Jiménez between 1898 and 1958.

SECONDARY SOURCES

ALBERTI, RAFAEL. *Imagen primera de...Juan Ramón Jiménez* (el al.).
    Losada, 1945. Important commentary on the influence of Jiménez
    on the author's generation of poets.
ASOMANTE, XIII, no. 2 (San Juan, Puerto Rico, 1957). Number devoted
    to Juan Ramón Jiménez.
BLY, ROBERT. *Juan Ramón Jiménez: Forty Poems*. Madison, Wisconsin:
    Sixties, 1967.
_____ *Lorca and Jiménez, Selected Poems*. Boston: Beacon, 1973. Bly's
    translations in both collections are generally commendable.
BO, CARLO. *La poesía con Juan Ramón*. Firenze: Edizioni di
    Revoluzioni, 1941. A perceptive analysis of Jiménez' poetry.
BROGGINI, NILDA ELENA. *Platero y yo, estudio estilístico*. Buenos Aires:
    Huemul, 1963. A stylistic study of *Platero*. Conventional criticism.
CARACOLA, nos. 60-61 (Malaga, 1957). Number devoted to Juan Ramón
    Jiménez.
CERNUDA, LUIS. *Estudios sobre poesía española contemporánea*.
    Madrid: Guadarrama, 1957. For Jiménez, see pp. 121-137. A rather
    negative appraisal of Jiménez' poetry. Subjective.
CLAVILEÑO, VII, no. 42 (Madrid, 1957). Number devoted to Juan
    Ramón Jiménez.
COLE, LEO R. *The Religious Instinct in the Poetry of Juan Ramón
    Jiménez*. Oxford: Dolphin, 1967. A good study of Jiménez' work
    considered from religious, philosophical and esthetic points of view.

CORREA, GUSTAVO. *Poesía española del siglo veinte.* New York: Appleton-Century-Crofts, 1972. An anthology with a representative selection of Jiménez' poetry, biographical and critical commentary, and a substantial bibliography.

DEL SAZ OROZCO, CARLOS. *El concepto de dios en Juan Ramón Jiménez.* Madrid: Razón y Fe, 1963. A well-documented and fair exposition of Jiménez' religious evolution as expressed in his work.

DÍAZ PLAJA, GUILLERMO. *Juan Ramón Jiménez en su poesía.* Madrid: Aguilar, 1958. Overall view of Jiménez' work. Sketchy.

DÍEZ CANEDO, ENRIQUE. *Juan Ramón Jiménez en su obra.* México: El colegio de México, 1944. Jiménez' poetic evolution. Brief but fair critical evaluation.

FIGUEIRA, GASTÓN. *Juan Ramón Jiménez. Poeta de lo inefable.* Montevideo: Biblioteca Alfar, 1944. Brief survey of Jiménez' poetry.

FOGELQUIST, DONALD F. "Juan Ramón Jiménez: Vida y obra, bibliografía, antología." *Revista Hispánica Moderna,* XXIV (April-July, 1958), nos. 2-3. Has an extensive bibliography.

FRENTE LITERARIO (Madrid), May 5, 1934. Number devoted to Juan Ramón Jiménez.

GARFIAS, FRANCISCO. *Juan Ramón Jiménez.* Madrid: Taurus, 1958. A conventional biographical and critical work. Interesting iconography.

GICOVATE, BERNARDO. *La poesía de Juan Ramón Jiménez.* San Juan de Puerto Rico: Asomante, 1959. A concise analysis of Jiménez' poetry. Good explanation of his technical evolution. Little comment on latest works.

GOMEZ DE LA SERNA, RAMÓN. *Retratos contemporáneos.* Buenos Aires: Editorial Sudamericana, 1941. Contains a brief but valuable biographical and critical study of Jiménez.

GUERRERO RUIZ, JUAN. *Juan Ramón de viva voz.* Madrid: Insula, 1961. The diary of a friend and apologist of Jiménez, covering the years 1913 to 1936. An important source of detailed information about Jiménez' life in Madrid.

GULLÓN, RICARDO. *Conversaciones con Juan Ramón.* Madrid: Taurus, 1958. A record of conversations between the author and Jiménez, 1952-1955. Some inaccuracies.

_____ *Estudios sobre Juan Ramón Jiménez.* Buenos Aires: Losada, 1960. Essays. Biography and criticism. Sound critical evaluation.

_____ *El último Juan Ramón.* Madrid: Alfaguara, 1968. A supplement to earlier biographies. Covers the last years of Jiménez' life in Puerto Rico.

HAYS, H. R. *The Selected Writings of Juan Ramón Jiménez*. A representative selection of Jiménez' poetry in English translation. Occasional inaccuracies.

INSULA, XII, nos. 128-129 (Madrid, 1957). Number devoted to Juan Ramón Jiménez.

LA TORRE, nos. 19-20 (San Juan, Puerto Rico, 1957). Number devoted to Juan Ramón Jiménez.

LIRA, OSVALDO. *Poesía y mística en Juan Ramón Jiménez*. Santiago, Chile: Editorial de la Universidad Católica, 1969. An extensive study of Jiménez' poetry as the expression of religious sentiment. Subjective.

NEDDERMANN, EMMY. *Die symbolistischen Stilelemente im Werke von Juan Ramón Jiménez*. Hamburg: Seminar Für Romanische Sprachen und Kultur, 1935. Symbolism in Jiménez' poetry. A valuable stylistic study.

OLSON, PAUL. *Circle of Paradox: Time and Essence in the Poetry of Juan Ramón Jiménez*. Baltimore: The Johns Hopkins Press, 1967. An intelligent and well-written analysis of the esthetic and philosophic bases of Jiménez' work.

PABLOS, BASILIO DE. *El tiempo en la poesía de Juan Ramón Jiménez*. Madrid: Gredos, 1965. A study of Jiménež' poetry in philosophical and religious context. Somewhat desultory.

PALAU DE NEMES, GRACIELA. *Vida y obra de Juan Ramón Jiménez*. Madrid: Gredos, 1957. The most complete biographical study of Jiménez. Substantial bibliography.

POESIA ESPAÑOLA, no. 60 (Madrid, 1956). Number devoted to Juan Ramón Jiménez.

POETRY, LXXXII, no. 4 (Chicago, 1953). Number devoted to Juan Ramón Jiménez.

PREDMORE, MICHAEL P. *La obra en prosa de Juan Ramón Jiménez*. Madrid: Gredos, 1966. An extensive and useful study of Jiménez' prose.

―――― *La poesía hermética de Juan Ramón Jiménez*. Madrid: Gredos, 1973. The *Diary* as a key to Jiménez' poetic expression. Interpretations of symbols raise some questions.

ROACH, ELOÏSE, trans. *Juan Ramón Jiménez: Three Hundred Poems*. Austin: University of Texas Press, 1957. A representative selection of Jiménez' poems competently translated. Occasional lapses.

―――― *Platero and I*. Austin: University of Texas Press, 1957. The most widely known translation of *Platero*.

ROBERTS, WILLIAM and MARY, trans. *Platero and I*. Oxford: The Dolphin Book Co., 1956. A sensitive and accurate translation. Drawings by Baltasar Lobo.

SALGADO, MARÍA ANTONIA. *El arte polifacético de las "caricaturas líricas" juanramonianas.* Madrid: Insula, 1968. A systematic study of the lyric caricatures as a genre. Limited to this minor aspect of Jiménez' work.

SÁNCHEZ BARBUDO, ANTONIO. *Cincuenta poemas comentados.* Madrid: Gredos, 1953. Commentaries on fifty poems of Jiménez' second period. Simple, direct interpretations.

―――― *Dios deseante y deseado.* Madrid: Aguilar, 1964. An important contribution to the study of Jiménez. Contains some previously unknown poems and gives explanatory comments on them.

―――― *La Segunda época de Juan Ramón Jiménez.* Madrid: Gredos, 1962. Brief commentaries on representative poems of Jiménez' "second" period and their unifying theme. Forthright criticism although not always conclusive.

SCHONBERG, JEAN-LOUIS. *Juan Ramón Jiménez, on le chant d'Orphée.* La Baconniére, 1961. An incisive critical study of Jiménez' poetry and prose.

TREND, J. B., trans. *Juan Ramón Jiménez. Fifty Spanish Poems.* New York: Oxford University Press, 1950; Berkeley and Los Angeles: University of California, 1951. An introductory essay on Jiménez and English translations of fifty of his poems. Many deviations from the original.

ULIBARRÍ, SABINE R. *El mundo poético de Juan Ramón.* Madrid: Edhigar, S. L. 1962. A commentary on stylistic features and symbols in Jiméne' poetry.

YOUNG, HOWARD T. *The Victorious Expression.* Madison: The University of Wisconsin Press, 1964. For Jiménez, see pp. 77-137. A concise, but careful and perceptive analysis of Jiménez' work.

ZARDOYA, CONCHA. "El dios deseado y deseante de Juan Ramón Jiménez." In *Poesía española contemporánea.* Madrid: Guadarrama, 1961, pp. 219-240. A useful study of *Animal of Depth* and *Desired and Desiring God* in the context of contemporary Spanish poetry.

Index